500 HR Certification Practice Questions With Explanations: PHR, SPHR, SHRM-CP, SHRM-SCP.

Olamide Asekun, PHR.

2016 Edition.

ALL RIGHTS RESERVED.

No part of this publication may be reproduced, stored in a retrieval system or transmitted in any form or by any means, electronic, mechanical, photocopying, recording, scanning or otherwise, except as permitted under Section 107 or 108 of the 1976 United States Copyright Act, without the prior written permission of the Author.

DISCLAIMER OF WARRANTY: WHILE THE PUBLISHER AND AUTHOR HAVE USED THEIR BEST EFFORTS IN PUTTING TOGETHER THIS BOOK, THEY MAKE NO WARRANTIES WITH RESPECT TO THE ACCURACY OR COMPLETENESS OF THE CONTENTS OF THIS BOOK AND SPECIFICALLY DISCLAIM ANY IMPLIED WARRANTIES FOR ANY PARTICULAR PURPOSE. NEITHER THE PUBLISHER NOT THE AUTHOR SHALL BE LIABLE FOR DAMAGES ARISING HEREFROM.

Purpose of This Book.

This book provides accurate information and explanation of questions regarding the HR exams in the title above, within the timeframe of its publication.

The federal and state laws discussed in this book are subject to revisions, amendments and judicial revisions that may affect employer or employee laws, rights and obligations.

All rights reserved Copyright 2016.

Introduction.

This book will help you immensely in your PHR, SPHR and SHRM-CP exam preparations as explanations for each answer have been included.

The alternatives in the multiple-choice questions have been carefully selected, please review the alternatives and seek to understand each one.

The questions have been separated into 5 sections, each consisting of 100 questions. You will find the answers and explanations to the questions at the end of each of the 5 sections.

There are tons of questions with "except" which seeks to know if you have adequate knowledge of the subject matter **AND what doesn't pertain to it.**

Again, Don't skip over the alternatives; read and painstakingly go through the process of understanding the entire question.

The following are exam tips that will serve a candidate well;

1. Read the question twice. Don't be in a hurry. Reading a second time will reveal some critical word that you passed over initially.

2. Calm down and take your mind off the exam for a minute then bring it back. You need a fresh perspective to answer the questions correctly and clearing your mind intermittently will help you achieve this.

3. Use a variety of study resources. Use a study guide, videos, practice questions and exam simulation systems but don't fall into information paralysis. Streamline your resources and focus on the study resources you have chosen but by all means, engage your mental, visual and auditory learning processes.

4. Check for words like "not", "except", "most likely", "least likely", "voluntary", "involuntary". Noting these terms in a question is critical to selecting the right answer.

5. Remember that an answer choice may be true and a fact but not the accurate answer. Be alert and prepared to answer the question, not necessarily identify a fact.

6. Prepare for real world HR experiential questions, so study with resources that provide knowledge of HR experience in the USA. Corporate HR webinars will help in this regard.

7. I put together a blog called **passphr.blogspot.com** with loads of exam success tips. Please check it out. It will prove useful in your preparations.

8. Pray and ask God for favour, commit your exams into the hands of the Lord Jesus. Please note, prayer does not take the place of hardwork and diligence.

9. Do not be slothful, read overnight, put aside distractions and discipline yourself.

I wish you success!

Olamide Asekun.

Section 1 Questions

1. Which of the following communications is an employer legally required to inform employees?
   a. Affirmative Action Plan as required by the OFCCP.
   b. Cost-of-Living-Adjustment (COLA) responsibilities.
   c. When WARN applies in the case of a mass layoff or plant closing.
   d. Tax information on Independent contractors.

2. Shewa earns an hourly rate of $12 and worked 47 hours in the 14th workweek. Shewa is to receive a one-time $30 holiday bonus, she is also entitled to $10 as a weekly perfect attendance bonus. With the information given, how much is Shewa's total weekly compensation for the 14th workweek?
   a. $646.74.
   b. $646.
   c. $616.12.
   d. 616.

3. Which of the following occurs if an employee comes to work in an inappropriate attire and is promptly sent home to change clothes?
   a. Negative reinforcement.
   b. Punishment.
   c. Extinction.
   d. Positive reinforcement.

4. Tim works in Ohio where the state minimum wage is $8.00. However, his company pays him $7.25 which is the current federal minimum wage. Tim's friend, Ann tells him this is illegal. Is Ann right?
   a. Yes, the minimum wage payable to Tim is the state minimum wage because he is a resident of Ohio.
   b. No, The federal minimum wage prevails over the state minimum wage always.
   c. Yes, the higher minimum wage prevails when considering either the federal or the state minimum wage.
   d. No, Tim is an exempt employee and exempted from minimum wage pay.

5. What is the formula for calculating turnover rates in an organisation according to the Department of Labor?
   a. (Total Terminations x 100) / (Avg. Number of Employees)
   b. (Number of Terminations x 10/ (Avg. Number of Employees)
   c. (Avg. Number of Employees) / (Number of Terminations)
   d. (Avg. Number of Employees) / (Number of Terminations x 10)

6. Most FLSA exemptions have the salary requirement of $455 per week, which of the following exemptions do not require a salary requirement?
   a. Computer professional exemption.
   b. Learned professional exemption.

c. Outside sales exemption.
d. Administrative exemption.

7. Unemployment benefits are paid by the ------- government to workers who have become unemployed through no fault of their own. These benefits are funded by federal and state unemployment taxes levied against employers.
a. State.
b. Federal.
c. Local.
d. County.

8. Which of the following is another name for an Ishikawa diagram?
a. Bell Curve.
b. Pareto Diagram.
c. Cause and Effect Diagram.
d. None of the above.

9. The Halz company has 300 employees and intends to lay off 100 employees due to redundancy. The HR Manager is debating whether the WARN Act applies to this layoff. Does it?
a. No, WARN applies to layoffs of at least 500 employees.
b. No, WARN applies to companies that have a total of 500 employees.
c. Yes, WARN applies to mass layoffs where 33% of the workforce will be laid off.
d. Yes, WARN applies to companies that have a minimum of 200 employees.

10. Ann, a HR professional has discovered green circle employees and intends to correct this to avoid discrimination claims as other employees in the same job are paid in the correct range. What is a green circle employee?
a. An employee covered under the 5 protected classes by Title VII.
b. An employee that is paid above the maximum salary range for the job position.
c. An employee that is paid under the minimum salary range for the job position.
d. An employee that is not entitled to restricted stock.

11. What class of employers are exempt from keeping OSHA records of employee occupational injury and illness?
a. Employers with ten or fewer employees
b. Low hazard industries.
c. Employers in the educational sector.
d. A and B.

12. Due to a layoff of 20% of its employees, the CEO of Nikky Jones Inc. has instructed the HR Manager to provide services to help smooth the transition for the exiting employees. These services can best be described as?
a. Severance packages.
b. Layoff benefits.
c. Outplacement services.
d. Unemployment Insurance.

13. Two of your employees cannot work as full-time employees anymore, one has a disabled son and another has begun a budding business. They have decided to share the duties of a full-time position between themselves, this is an example of?
a. Part-time employees.
b. Telecommuting.
c. Contingent Workforce.
d. Job sharing.

14. Workers' compensation generally covers the following except?
a. Wage replacement benefits.
b. Medical treatment
c. Vocational rehabilitation.
d. Restricted stock.

15. The federal program that provides aid to workers who lose their jobs or whose hours of work and wages are reduced as a result of increased imports is called?
a. Workforce Investment Act.
b. Trade Adjustment Assistance Program.
c. Unemployment Assistance Program.
d. Readjustment Assistance Program.

16. Which of the following organizations should employers contact for information about substances used in work processes to determine whether or not they are toxic?
a. Equal Employment Opportunity Commission.
b. National Institute for Occupational Safety and Health.
c. Occupational Health and Safety Administration.
d. Department of Labor.

17. Ted had his wages recently garnished for child support payments. Ted has a wife and children aside from the child for whom he is to pay child support. What is the maximum child support payments that can be garnished from Ted's wages?
a. 25% of Ted's wages before legally mandated deductions.
b. 50% of Ted's wages after legally mandated deductions.
c. 60% of Ted's wages after legally mandated deductions.
d. 25% of Ted's wages after legally mandated deductions.

18. The Clips company recently acquired the Line enterprises. A major concern for the CEO of the Clips company is how to retain the executives of the Line enterprises. Which of the following should the HR Manager of the Clips company recommend?
a. Gold Parachute.
b. Golden Handshake.
c. Golden Handcuffs.
d. Golden Life Jacket.

19. Jean has been offered an executive role at a Software engineering firm. She is concerned though about the stock options offered her which will not vest until she has been with the company for 10 years, and agreements that state she must return certain

bonuses if she leaves the company before 5 years. The benefits stated above are most likely?
a. Executive pay trends.
b. Golden Parachutes.
c. Golden Handcuffs.
d. Qualified stock options.

20. Which of the following is not included in the OSHA general duty clause?
a. Employers are to provide a place of employment free from recognized hazards.
b. Employers are to comply with occupational safety and health standards.
c. Employees are to comply with occupational safety and health standards.
d. Employees are required to take workplace violence prevention training.

21. For training that requires practical understanding of a realistic business situation, which of the following instructional methods is best?
a. Virtual training.
b. Case study.
c. Conference.
d. Presentation.

22. A clause which prevents the reopening of collective bargaining negotiations during the term of the contract is called?
a. Closed clause.
b. Prevention clause.
c. Zipper clause.
d. Union clause.

23. Wayne, the CEO of Wane company is searching for a performance program that clearly indicates to employees that performance impacts rewards. What kind of compensation program is this?
a. Internal equity compensation program.
b. Total-rewards compensation program.
c. Line of sight compensation program.
d. Entitlement compensation program.

24. Which group has authority over unfair labor practices for federal employees?
a. National Arbitration Board.
b. National Labor Relations Board.
c. Federal Labor Board.
d. Federal Labor Relations Authority.

25. Sandra's employer refuses to offer her light duty during her pregnancy as the Pregnancy Discrimination Act (PDA) states that Sandra be treated as any other employee. Is this accurate?
a. Yes, that is an exact statement from the PDA.
b. No, the PDA states pregnant employees be treated the same as any other employee with a short-term disability.
c. Yes, the PDA is not the same as the ADA.

d. None of the above.

26. Which of the following will help you determine if a measurement actually measures something that cannot be directly observed?
a. Content validity.
b. Construct validity.
c. Concurrent validity.
d. Predictive validity.

27. The ADEA and the FLSA require that payroll records be kept for how long?
a. 3 years for exempt employees.
b. 4.5 years.
c. 2 years.
d. 3 years for all employees.

28. With regards to affirmative action, comparison of incumbency to availability means?
a. The availability of a particular protected group in the organisation.
b. Protected class in job groups in relation to availability in labor pool.
c. Demographic data on the labor pool.
d. Modification of current employment practices.

29. The Dante company evaluates jobs by identifying and benchmarking job positions, with an emphasis on internal equity. This method of job evaluation is called?
a. Factor-point method
b. Classification Method.
c. Rating Method.
d. Ranking Method.

30. Your Head of IT has received complaints from his team members with similar responsibilities who claim that there is a wide disparity in their respective base pay. As the HR Business Partner, which of the following is likely to be the issue?
a. Distributive justice
b. Procedural justice.
c. Lack of equity pay.
d. Lack of pay equity.

31. In conducting a needs assessment for a payroll system in your organisation, which of the following should be your first step?
a. Identify organizational needs.
b. Compare various independent contractors and their rates.
c. Determine the payroll system of competitors.
d. None of the above.

32. Which of the following is not a statutory deduction?
a. Medicare.
b. Income tax.
c. Wage garnishment.

d. Employee Stock Purchase Plans (ESPP).

33. The Binc company is not certain on how to process three wage garnishment orders for Ned, an employee in the Sales department who receives 25% of his base pay in commission. How should the wage garnishment orders be processed?
a. Fire Ned, the Consumer Credit Protection Act doesn't protect employees that have more than one wage garnishment order.
b. Process all of the court-ordered garnishments.
c. Process no more than 25% of Ned's gross income.
d. Process no more than 25% of Ned's disposable income.

34. The business management tool that focuses on 4 key areas; financial results, customer results, internal business processes and learning & innovation is called?
a. Six Sigma.
b. Balanced scorecard.
c. Management by Objectives.
d. Total Quality Management.

35. Which of the following is not one of the five phases of a project?
a. Planning
b. Budgeting.
c. Controlling.
d. Closing.

36. Your company receives a court order to garnish Fred's wages for unpaid child support. Can Fred be terminated for a child support wage garnishment order?
a. No, Title III prohibits termination if pay is garnished for only one debt.
b. Yes, Title III does not prohibit termination for any wage garnishment.
c. Yes, Employees are under the employment at-will doctrine and can be terminated for no cause.
d. No, Fred can only be terminated if the wage garnishment is for child neglect.

37. Which law states that the statute of limitations (period within which legal action can be brought) for pay discrimination lawsuits resets every time an allegedly discriminatory paycheck is issued?
a. Equal Pay Act.
b. Workplace Anti-Discrimination Act
c. Wagner Act
d. Lilly Ledbetter Fair Pay Act.

38. What is the key differentiating factor to determine whether an individual is an employee or an independent contractor?
a. If the employer pays bonuses to the individual.
b. The degree of control over the work processes by the employer.
c. If the individual works in the employer's business location.
d. If the individual is exempt under the FLSA.

39. Which of the following is not a requirement by the Employee Retirement Income Security Act of 1974 (ERISA) ?
   a. Private employers must set up a retirement plan and ensure all full-time employees are participants.
   b. Employers are to provide participants with information about health & pension plans called the Summary Plan Description (SPD).
   c. Fiduciary accountability.
   d. Participants have the right to sue for benefits.

40. Allen has analyzed an employee's base salary in comparison with the midpoint of the company's salary range. He divided the employee's base pay of $50,000 by the midpoint which is $60,000 and multiplied this by 100 to get a percentage. Allen determines that the percentage is 83.3%. What is Allen calculating?
   a. Regression Analysis.
   b. Salary Adjustment.
   c. Compa-ratio.
   d. Merit increase matrix.

41. Tope will not receive her any of her employer's contribution to her pension plan till she has worked for the employer for 5 years. This is what type of vesting?
   a. Graded vesting.
   b. Immediate vesting.
   c. Cliff vesting.
   d. Participant vesting.

42. In labor relations, the peer-review panel procedure is a function of:
   a. Harassment escalation.
   b. Promissory estoppel.
   c. Conflict resolution.
   d. Union organizing.

43. The EEOC makes many records publicly available on its website but will not release confidential records. Which of the following is not a confidential record?
   a. An employer's EEO report.
   b. Social Security numbers.
   c. Records that reflect EEOC's internal decision-making.
   d. Guidance documents.

44. A voluntary resolution practice used by the EEOC for resolving charges of discrimination is called?
   a. Witness interviews.
   b. Mediation.
   c. Litigation.
   d. Constructive discharge.

45. Which of the following employment laws does not require the employer to place a poster of the laws in a conspicuous location in the workplace?

a. Equal Employment Opportunity Commission (EEOC).
b. Fair Labor Standard Act (FLSA).
c. Occupational Safety and Health Act (OSHA).
d. None of the above.

46. The Labor Management Relations Act is also known as which of the following Acts;
a. Landrum-Griffith Act.
b. Taft-Hartley Act.
c. Wagner Act.
d. Norris-LaGuardia Act.

47. Which of the following are exceptions to the definition of discrimination in the workplace?
a. Essential job functions & BFOQs.
b. Merit systems.
c. Piece-rate systems.
d. All of the above.

48. Which of the following is not an Unfair Labor Practice by an employer?
a. Refusal to bargain.
b. Discrimination on the basis of labor activity.
c. Discrimination in retaliation for going to the NLRB.
d. Threats of bodily injury to non-striking employees.

49. Tayo has questions about labor union officer elections, union financial practices and transparency in labor union operations. Which of the following agencies should she contact?
a. EEOC.
b. NLRB.
c. Office of Labor Management Standard.
d. Wage and Hour Division of the DOL.

50. The first step in the process for an election to bring in a union is?
a. Decertification.
b. Union organizing.
c. Petition Filing.
d. Deauthorization.

51. Vinney is to calculate the turnover rate in the Yen company. The number of employees that have left are 500 while the total number of employees are 1,500. What is the turnover rate for the Yen company?
a. 83.3%
b. 33.3%.
c. 25%.
d. 45%.

52. Which of the following is not an example of indirect compensation?
a. Variable compensation.
b. Insurance premiums.

c. Company car.
d. FMLA benefits.

53. For an employee to qualify under the administrative exemption of the Fair Labor Standards Act, one of the requirements is;
a. The primary duty requires creative endeavour.
b. The primary duty requires office work directly related to general business operations.
c. The primary duty is managing the organization with discretion and independent judgement.
d. All of the above.

54. The union of the Acme company is on strike. The union has informed the Edge company, a major supplier to the Acme company, that their supply truck will not be given access to the Acme company's factories during the period of the strike. What is happening here?
a. A skip-level strike.
b. A secondary boycott.
c. A primary boycott.
d. An economic boycott.

55. Your company has an agreement with Jane a marketing employee, that as a condition of employment she is not to be a member of a labor union. This is a violation of which of the following acts?
a. The National Labor Relations Act.
b. The Sherman Antitrust Act.
c. The Norris-La Guardia Act.
d. The Wagner Act.

56. Title VII of the Civil Rights Act protects the following except?
a. Age.
b. Race.
c. Color.
d. Sex.

57. A survey that requires information on specific skillsets or competitors that may not be readily available on generic surveys is called?
a. Employee survey.
b. Commissioned survey.
c. Retention survey.
d. Salary survey.

58. What are the sequence of steps for a progressive disciplinary process?
a. Verbal warning, written warning, final warning, suspension, termination.
b. Written warning, Performance improvement plan, suspension.
c. Verbal warning, written warning, termination.
d. Verbal warning, written warning, termination for fiduciary offenses.

59. Malcolm Knowles' study on andragogy (the study of how adults learn) described 5 characteristics. Which of the following is not one of them?
a. Motivation to learn.
b. Readiness to learn.
c. Orientation to learning
d. Kinesthetic learning.

60. Which of the following is not a characteristic of an independent contractor?
a. Pension plans.
b. Work schedule flexibility.
c. Expenses are reimbursed.
d. Owns work tools.

61. The ADA states that individuals covered by the act;
a. Can be discriminated against if there is a valid BFOQ.
b. Must request for an accommodation.
c. Must be able to perform all duties of the job with or without accommodation.
d. Must be able to perform the essential job functions.

62. Which of the following recruitment methods allows candidates to talk to employers about an opening without making a formal job proposition?
a. Job fairs.
b. Video Interviews.
c. Employment agencies.
d. Web applications.

63. Which of the following is not an example of internal recruitment strategy?
a. Job enlargement.
b. Job posting.
c. Transfers.
d. Promotions.

64. The following are illegal under the ADA except?
a. Ask an applicant whether he/she is disabled.
b. To require the applicant to take a medical examination before making a job offer.
c. Ask an applicant questions about ability to perform job-related functions.
d. Require an individual with a disability to accept an accommodation that is not needed.

65. Which of the following is not a benefit of training?
a. To increase company liability.
b. Productivity improvements.
c. Improved morale.
d. Remain competitive.

66. The following are advantages of zero-based budgeting except?
a. Requires managers to justify every dollar they plan to spend.
b. Promotes efficiency.
c. Eliminates Redundancy.

d. Short term planning bias.

67. The process by which a neutral third party assists negotiators (in a non-binding process) in their discussions and also suggests settlement proposals is known as:
a. Arbitration.
b. Mediation.
c. Constructive confrontation.
d. Reconciliation.

68. What is a consent election?
a. When the regional director schedules a hearing to resolve election disputes.
b. An order by the NLRB to cancel the election.
c. An agreement between an employer & the union to waive the pre-election hearing.
d. A directed election approved by the NLRB.

69. According to OSHA, a recordable case is one in which:
a. Was caused by common cold.
b. Injury where first-aid is administered.
c. Injury results in days away from work.
d. Injury occurring on commute to work.

70. A Safety Data Sheets (SDS) is required:
a. When the employment facility is located in the path of hazardous material transportation.
b. For each hazardous chemical that is used, processed, or stored.
c. From any employee handling hazardous materials.
d. For each employee hired into a position that has exposure to hazardous materials.

71. A Polygraph test can be administered in which of the following circumstances?
a. To a bankrupt employee.
b. To all fiduciaries of pension plans.
c. An employee is suspected of embezzlement of spousal support.
d. An employee is suspected of industrial espionage in the workplace.

72. Which of the following is NOT a ergonomic injury?
a. Teratogens.
b. Repetitive Stress Injury.
c. Musculoskeletal disorders.
d. Cumulative Trauma Injuries.

73. The following assumptions are true about the Kirkpatrick's Results level evaluation except?
a. Training results in reduced costs.
b. Improvement of the bottom line.
c. Increase in knowledge and skills.
d. Increased production.

74. Which of the following is not a characteristic of stress in the workplace?

a. 50% of all adults suffer adverse effects from stress.
b. Stress management techniques increase employee negligence.
c. 75% of all physician office visits are for stress-related ailments.
d. Stress costs U.S. industry more than $300 billion dollars per year.

75. If an employee is earning a pay rate that is excessive compared to their counterparts of equal ability, this is identified as?
a. Red circle.
b. Compa-ratio.
c. Green circle.
d. Hour compression.

76. Which of the following would not be considered a major objective of Organizational Development?
a. Determining if the handbook is a business necessity.
b. Increase the level of interpersonal trust.
c. Increase employees' level of satisfaction.
d. Create conditions in which conflict is effectively managed.

77. Which of the following is likely to yield the highest level of participant retention?
a. Revision.
b. Application.
c. Discussion.
d. None of the above.

78. Learning organizations facilitate the learning of its members and transforms itself. Which of the following characteristics of a learning organization refers to deep-seated beliefs that color how we perceive and understand the world around us?
a. Systems thinking.
b. Mental models.
c. Personal mastery.
d. Team learning.

79. A management system that involves the use of strategy, data and employee involvement to increase the level of quality in order to meet customer needs is called?
a. Total Quality Management.
b. Quality planning.
c. Analytical tools.
d. Reengineering.

80. Which of these is NOT one of three barriers identified by the Glass Ceiling Act that prevents women and minorities from advancing to senior managerial levels?
a. Governmental Barriers.
b. Cultural Barriers.
c. Internal structural Barriers.
d. Societal Barriers.

81. During the mediation process, at which point will the mediator facilitate negotiations for the parties to come to agreement?
a. Structure.
b. Negotiating.
c. Options.
d. Fact-finding.

82. An arbitrator who is selected to serve for the life of the contract to hear all disputes that arise is called?
a. An ad hoc arbitrator.
b. A permanent arbitrator.
c. A neutral arbitrator.
d. A tripartite arbitration panel.

83. A demotion, reassignment to menial or degrading work or involuntary transfer to a less desirable position can lead to which of the following?
a. Constructive discharge claim.
b. Progressive discipline.
c. Redundancy.
d. Resignation.

84. Dan's manager wants to fire him for poor performance. However, the HR manager is against Dan being fired. Which of the following is NOT a valid reason for not firing Dan?
a. Dan cannot be fired for his race, color, sex, national origin or religion.
b. Dan cannot be fired for retaliation or whistleblowing.
c. Dan cannot be fired for wage garnishment of only one debt.
d. Dan cannot be fired because he is protected by WARN.

85. A leadership style that focuses on results and offering rewards in exchange for accomplishing organizational goals is called?
a. Coaching.
b. Transactional.
c. Transformational.
d. Quid pro quo.

86. A union negotiates with one employer, then uses the gains made from the initial negotiation as a basis for negotiating with the next employer. This is known as;
a. Point-factor bargaining.
b. Multi-unit bargaining.
c. Leapfrogging.
d. Multi-employer bargaining.

87. The Act that increased reporting requirements for pension plans, required that pension funds be separated from operating funds, established vesting schedules and fiduciary standards of fund management is called;
a. A cash balance plan.
b. A ROTH IRA.
c. ERISA.

d. OBRA.

88. An employee at your organisation has not shown up to work for a week and has not contacted his manager either. What is the most appropriate next step for HR to take?
a. Send him a letter of suspension.
b. Call his spouse who is his next of kin.
c. Make enquiries to determine if the absence is for a reason protected by law e.g. FMLA.
d. Terminate the employee for no-call, no-show.

89. The Labor Management Relations Act is also known as?
a. The Taft-Hartley Act.
b. The Wagner Act.
c. The Railway Labor Act.
d. None of the Above.

90. Which of the following is not a form of alternative dispute resolution?
a. Arbitration.
b. Mediation.
c. Constructive confrontation.
d. Bargaining.

91. A company that wants to encourage a union-free workplace should implement which of the following?
a. Pension and healthcare benefits.
b. Union organizing assessments.
c. Ensure open communication between employees and leadership.
d. Investigate employees who have been in unions in previous jobs.

92. The Labor Management Reporting Disclosure Act (LMRDA) promotes union democracy and financial integrity through standards for union elections/trusteeships and safeguards for union assets. The group that would most likely investigate a violation of the LMRDA would be?
a. Office of Labor Management Standards.
b. Department of Justice.
c. Federal Labor Investigation Board.
d. National Labor Standards Board

93. A temporary group of people formed to carry out a specific mission or project, or to solve a single problem that requires a multidisciplinary approach is called?
a. Committee.
b. Suggestion group.
c. Task force.
d. Focus group.

94. The statement, "The more hours I spend at the office, the less time I spend with my family" is an example of which of the following?
a. Quantitative analysis

b. Negative correlation.
c. Positive correlation.
d. Linear Regression.

95. The point-factor and Hay system of job evaluations are of what method?
a. Rating method.
b. Classification method.
c. Coefficient method.
d. Ranking method.

96. Ted, a new employee is being paid $5,000 extra in his base pay than his colleagues who have been with the company for 5 years or more. This is best described as?
a. Procedural justice.
b. Wage compression.
c. Distributive justice.
d. Green circle.

97. Base salary is divided by the midpoint of the salary range then multiplied by 100. This is a formula for?
a. Midpoint progression.
b. Compa-ratio.
c. Disparate pay.
d. COLA ratio.

98. When an employee works more hours, his paycheck increases proportionately. This is an example of?
a. Delphi technique.
b. Nominal statement.
c. Simulation Model.
d. Positive correlation.

99. Tina has been asked to brainstorm on the costs and value of a project with regard to expanding the business. Which of the following will be the best option for Tina?
a. Cost-benefit analysis.
b. Return on Investment.
c. Business Impact.
d. Result measurement.

100. Ezekiel has to change his work schedule to an earlier closing time three days a week. Which alternate work schedule is best for Ezekiel?
a. Job sharing.
b. Flex-time.
c. Temporary employment.
d. Termination.

Section 1 Answers and Explanations

500 HR Certification Questions.

1. **C.** The Worker Adjustment and Retraining Notification (WARN) requires a 60 days advance notice to be given to employees and their union representatives in a mass layoff or plant closing.

2. **A.** Shewa is entitled to overtime pay because she worked more than 40 hours in the workweek. Remember that non-discretionary bonuses will be included to calculate overtime pay. Step 1: calculate Shewa's regular pay (total pay+additional compensation)=($12*47)+ $10 = $564+ $10 = $574; Step 2: calculate Shewa's regular rate of pay (regular pay divided by total hours worked)=$574/47 = $12.21; Step 3: calculate Shewa's overtime pay (regular rate of pay*0.5*(hours worked-40 hours) = $12.21*0.5*(47-40) = $12.21*0.5*7 = $42.74; Step 4: Total weekly compensation = $564 (being her total pay) + $30 (being her holiday bonus) + $10 (being her perfect attendance bonus) + $42.74 (being her overtime pay in which the non-discretionary $10 bonus was included) = $646.74. Even though Shewa is to earn $564 ($12*47 hours) as her regular pay, because the $10 perfect attendance bonus is not a one-time incentive and is dependent on her hours worked, it must be factored into her overtime pay calculations. Please note that the holiday bonus was not included to calculate the overtime pay because it is a one-time bonus and discretionary.

3. **B.** Punishment is a process by which a consequence immediately follows a behavior which decreases the likelihood of repetition. This is from B.F. Skinner's theory of operant conditioning which entails changing behavior by the use of reinforcement.

4. **C.** When determining what minimum wage to pay between the federal and state minimum wage, the higher rate supersedes the lower rate. Tim should be paid the higher rate of $8.00.

5. **A.** Turnover formula: <u>Number of employees who left during the given time period</u> x 100
   Average number of employees during the given time period.

6. **C.** The outside sales exemption is the only exemption that does not require the salary requirement of $455 per week or $23,660 annually. Please note that effective **December 1, 2016**, there shall be an increase in the salary requirements for an exempt employee;(from $455 to $913 per week; from $23,660 to $47,476 annually) and Highly Compensated Employees (HCE) total annual compensation requirement (from $100,000 to $134,004 per year).

7. **A.** Unemployment benefits are generally paid by state governments.

8. **C.** The Ishikawa diagram created by Kaoru Ishikawa is also called the cause and effect diagram or the fishbone diagram. It helps identify many possible causes for an effect or problem.

9. **C.** The Worker Adjustment and Retraining Notification (WARN) Act of 1988 applies to mass layoffs and plant closings, requiring a 60-days advance notice to workers. A mass layoff is one where 500 employees OR 33% of the workforce (consisting of at least 50 employees) will be laid off. 33% of 300 employees is 99, so WARN applies to the Halz company's planned layoff.

10. **C.** A green circle employee is an employee that is paid below the minimum salary range for the job position. The green circle employee is paid less than the job is worth to the company. Red circle employees, the opposite, are paid over the maximum salary range established for the job positions.

11. **D.** There are two classes of employers that are exempt from keeping OSHA records; employers with 10 or fewer employees and low hazard industries.

12. **C.** Outplacement services are designed to make career transition easier for laid off employees, These services could be employee counseling, career guidance, resume writing and job placement help and events.

13. **D.** Job sharing is an alternative staffing method that allows two employees to share the responsibilities of a job.

14. D. *Workers' compensation provides compensation to employees who suffer job-related injuries and illnesses. Benefits do not include restricted stock which are company stock issued to executives, the stock is not fully transferable to them until certain conditions have been met.*

15. B. *The Trade Adjustment Assistance (TAA) program offers benefits and reemployment services to help unemployed workers who lose their jobs as a result of increased imports. Workers may be eligible for training, job search and relocation allowances, income support, and other reemployment services.*

16. B. *The National Institute for Occupational Safety and Health (NIOSH) is the federal agency responsible for conducting research and making recommendations for the prevention of work-related injury and illness.*

17. B. *Child support (and alimony) garnishments can be up to 50% of disposable earnings if the employee is supporting a spouse or child. If the employee is not supporting a spouse or child, up to 60% of disposable earnings can be garnished. An additional 5 percent may be garnished for support payments more than 12 weeks in arrears. Disposable earnings are earnings after legally mandated deductions (Social Security, Medicare) have been made. Other debts can be garnished up to 25% of disposable earnings.*

18. D. *Golden Life Jacket (also called stay bonus) is part of a compensation package that is offered to top executives of a company that is being acquired by another company. The purpose of this offer is to retain the executives in their current roles. These could be large bonuses or company stock options.*

19. C. *Golden handcuffs are offered by employers as a means of holding onto key employees and increasing employee retention.*

20. D. *The OSHA general duty clause does not include a requirement to take workplace violence prevention training.*

21. B. *Case studies are descriptions of a real life experience which are used to conduct trainings and enhance the participants' understanding and learning experience.*

22. C. *A zipper clause in the collective bargaining contract means that both parties waive the right to bargain during the term of the contract. Zipper clauses should be "clear and unmistakable."*

23. C. *Line of sight is a compensation program based on the premise where employees can clearly see that their performance impacts their pay.*

24. D. *The Federal Labor Relations Authority is an independent agency of the United States government that governs labor relations between the federal government and its employees.*

25. B. *The Pregnancy Discrimination Act of 1978 states that pregnant employees receive the same treatment as employees with any other short-term disability.*

26. B. *Construct validity refers to the degree to which a test or other measure assesses the theoretical construct it is supposed to measure. Content validity measures the significant parts or contents of the job e.g. a practical driving test for a truck driver role.*

27. D. *The Age Discrimination in Employment Act(ADEA) and the Fair Labor Standards Act (FLSA) require that payroll records be kept for 3 years for all employees.*

28. B. *One of the Affirmative action plan components is comparison of incumbency to availability which compares protected classes employed in each job group with availability in the labor force within a reasonable recruiting area.*

29. B. *Jobs can be evaluated by two methods, the classification and ranking methods. The classification method evaluates jobs by identifying benchmark positions and determining internal equity. Internal equity means the value of a job relative to other jobs in the company.*

30. B. *Procedural justice is the perception of how fair the process of arriving at pay ranges are perceived to be. Distributive justice indicates how closely pay reflects performance. Pay equity is the means of eliminating race and sex discrimination from pay or wages. Equity pay is a form of non-cash compensation that offers a form of ownership interest in a company.*

31. A. *The first step to a needs assessment is identify the needs and describe objectives clearly before reviewing existing and collecting new data.*

32. D. *ESPPs are not legally required deductions.*

33. D. *Wage garnishments are deductions made to satisfy a debt and should not exceed 25% of an employee's disposable income. Disposable income is an employee's pay after legally required deductions have been made. Firing Ned, though an option, doesn't answer the question.*

34. B. *The balanced scorecard is the management tool that ties the outcomes of each department into one measurement system. It tracks information in 4 key areas as detailed on the question.*

35. B. *Budgeting is a management function, not a project phase.*

36. A. *A wage garnishment is a legal procedure through which some portion of a person's earnings is required to be withheld by an employer for the payment of a debt. Title III of the Consumer Credit Protection Act (CCPA) prohibits employers from terminating employees whose wages are garnished for one debt. We can assume from the information that Fred has only one wage garnishment order.*

37. D. *The Lilly Ledbetter Fair Pay Act (LLFPA) states that an employee has 180 days to sue from the last discriminatory paycheck received. Prior to the LFPA, the statute of limitations of 180 days began to run from when the discriminatory act occurred and expired when 180 days were up; with the LFPA, the 180 days period within which legal action can be taken resets with each new discriminatory paycheck. The employee can also collect back-pay for the last two years.*

38. B. *The degree of control an employer has over an individual's work processes is the key consideration in determining if he/she is an employee or an independent contractor.*

39. A. *ERISA does not require any employer to establish a pension plan. It only requires employers who establish plans to meet certain minimum standards.*

40. C. *Compa-ratio compares an employee's pay with the midpoint of the salary range. Compa-ratios are used to measure an employee's pay relative to the market average pay for his/her position for salary equity analyses. The salary range midpoint is usually 100% and here the compa-ratio for the employee's pay is 83.3% of the salary range midpoint.*

41. C. *Cliff vesting is when the employee becomes fully vested at a specified time rather than becoming partially vested in increasing amounts over an extended period of time (graded vesting). An example of "cliff vesting" is when an employee is fully vested in a pension plan after 5 years of full time service. An example of graded vesting could be a five-year schedule in which the employee receives 20 percent vesting each year.*

42. C. Conflict resolution can be an internal procedure, one of which is known as peer-review panel. A Peer Review panel is a problem-solving process where an employee takes a dispute to a group or panel of fellow employees and managers for a decision. The decision is not binding on the employee, and he/she would be able to seek relief in traditional forums for dispute resolution if dissatisfied with the decision.

43. D. EEOC guidance documents are in the public domain and generally accessible; this includes the coverage and compliance requirements of the EEOC as well as enforcement guidance.

44. B. At the start of an investigation of a discrimination charge, the EEOC will notify the employer of the charge within 10 days, then advise both the organization and the charging party if the charge is eligible for mediation and settlement. Mediation and settlement are voluntary resolutions.

45. D. All the employment laws listed in the options above require employers to have posters of the laws placed in a conspicuous location in the workplace.

46. B. The Taft-Hartley is also known as the Labor Management Relations Act (LMRA); the Landrum-Griffith Act is also known as the Labor Management Reporting and Disclosure Act (LMRDA); the Wagner Act is also called the National Labor Relations Act.

47. D. Option A through C are valid exceptions allowable under Title VII of the Civil Rights Act of 1964.

48. D. A threat of bodily injury to non-striking employees is a Union ULP not an Employer ULP. An employer will not threaten an employee who refuses to go on a strike.

49. C. The Office of Labor-Management Standards (OLMS) of the U.S. Department of Labor administers and enforces most provisions of the Labor-Management Reporting and Disclosure Act of 1959 (LMRDA). The LMRDA promotes union democracy, transparency and financial integrity in private sector labor unions through standards for union officer elections, union trusteeships and safeguards for union assets.

50. C. To start the election process for a union, a petition must be filed with the nearest NLRB Regional Office showing interest in the union from at least 30% of employees.

51. B. The turnover rate is calculated as number of separations divided by the average number of employees multiplied by 100. The answer in this case is 33.3%.

52. A. Indirect compensation is compensation not paid directly (non-monetary remuneration) to the employee. Variable compensation which is also known as pay for performance is paid directly to the employee.

53. B. The administrative exemption of the FLSA has two requirements; the primary duty of office work directly related to management or business operations and duties which require the use of discretion and independent judgement. The _executive_ exemption has the primary duty of managing the organization while the _creative_ professional exemption has the primary duty of artistic or creative endeavours.

54. B. A secondary boycott is when a union coerces a neutral employer to cease doing business with a primary employer. Secondary boycotts are unlawful labor practices as defined by the Labor Management Relations Act (LMRA) or the Taft-Hartley Act.

55. C. The Norris-La Guardia Act prohibits yellow-dog contracts which is any agreement, instigated by an employer, which prevents an employee from joining a union.

56. A. The Title VII of the Civil Rights Act has 5 protected classes; race, color, religion, national origin and sex. Age is protected by the ADEA, Age Discrimination in Employment Act of 1967 and Disability is protected by the ADA, Americans with Disabilities Act of 1990.

57. B. A commissioned survey is a type of salary survey that provides specific information about predetermined skillsets or competitors.

58. A. The following are the basic steps to administering progressive discipline; Verbal warning; First written warning; Final written warning; Suspension; Termination of Employment.

59. D. Malcolm Knowles described 5 characteristics of adult learning, these are Self-concept; Experience; Readiness to learn; Orientation to learning & Motivation to learn. Kinesthetic or tactile learning, on the other hand, is physical learning i.e. learners who use a sense of touch to memorise knowledge.

60. A. An independent contractor is a person who contracts to do work for another person according to his or her own processes and methods; he is not subject to another's control except for what is specified in a contract and he/she does not enjoy employee benefits such as pension plans.

61. D. An individual with a disability must be qualified to perform the essential functions of the job with or without reasonable accommodation, in order to be protected by the ADA. The ADA does not interfere with the right to hire the best qualified applicant.

62. A. A job fair is also called a career fair or career expo. A job fair is an event in which employers, recruiters, and schools give information to potential employees in an attempt to get a good feel on the work needed.

63. A. Job Rotation is the systematic movement of employees from one job to another within the organization as a way to achieve different human resources objectives such as orienting new employees, training employees, enhancing career development and preventing job boredom. It is not a recruitment strategy.

64. C. An employer has the right to ask an applicant (regardless of disability status) about his/her ability to perform essential job functions.

65. A. Option A is not a training benefit.

66. D. In zero-based budgeting, a company draws up its budget from scratch every year, requiring managers to justify every dollar they plan to spend. The advantages of zero-based budgeting are flexible budgets, lower costs and more disciplined execution, while the disadvantages are resource intensiveness and a bias towards short-term planning.

67. B. Mediation is non-binding and there is no power to impose a resolution. Arbitration is similar to the court process as parties provide testimonies, give evidence similar to a trial and arbitrators are similar to judges. In mediation, the process is a negotiation with the assistance of a neutral third party who simply helps to facilitate discussion and eventual resolution of the dispute.

68. C. A consent election is an election in which an employer and union agree to waive the pre-election hearing. Consent elections are generally held if there is no substantial issue in dispute between the employer and unions involved in a union representation case.

69. C. An injury is recordable if it results in any of the following: death, days away from work, restricted work or transfer to another job, medical treatment beyond first aid, or loss of consciousness.

70. B. A Safety Data Sheet (SDS) is a document that contains information on the potential hazards and how to work safely with a chemical product. A SDS is required to comply with the OSHA Hazard Communications

Standard. The SDS includes information such as the properties of each chemical; the physical, health, and environmental health hazards; protective measures; and safety precautions for handling, storing, and transporting the chemical.

71. D. The Employee Polygraph Protection Act prohibits private employers from using lie detector tests, either for pre-employment screening or during the course of employment. However, polygraph tests can be administered in certain circumstances ; those of security service firms, pharmaceutical manufacturers & distributors and certain employees of private firms who are reasonably suspected of involvement in a theft, embezzlement, etc., that resulted in specific economic loss or injury to the employer such as industrial espionage.

72. A. Ergonomic injuries are injuries caused by awkward postures, forceful strain, exposure to vibration, heat or cold. Teratogens are not ergonomic injuries but chemicals that can disturb the development of an embryo or fetus.

73. C. The Results level evaluation will determine tangible business results of the training process in terms of reduced cost, improved quality, increased production and effects on the bottom-line. An increase in knowledge and skills will be analysed at the Learning level evaluation.

74. B. Stress management techniques help employees cope with having to handle more than they are used to, professionally or personally. These techniques will _not_ increase but rather reduce employee negligence.

75. A. Red circle is when an employee's pay rate is above the established salary maximum for that position. Hence, the employee is usually not eligible for further base pay increases until the range maximum surpasses the employee's pay rate. A green circle employee is one whose pay rate is below the minimum of the established pay range for a specific job or pay grade.

76. A. Organization development (OD) is a systematic method dedicated to expanding the knowledge and effectiveness of people to accomplish more successful organizational change and performance. Option A is not an objective of OD.

77. B. Application results in the highest level of participant retention in training.

78. B. Mental models are deep-seated beliefs or thought processes that color perceptions about how the world works.

79. A. Total quality management (TQM) consists of organization-wide efforts designed to continuously improves an organization's ability to deliver high-quality products and services with the end goal of meeting customer needs.

80. B. The glass ceiling act established a commission which identified three barriers to women and minorities from getting into senior management positions. These are Societal barriers, Internal Structural barriers and Governmental Barriers.

81. B. The mediation process solves grievances with the aid of a mediator. It has the following steps; Structure, Introductions, Fact-finding, Options, Negotiating and Writing the Agreement. At the negotiating stage, alternatives are placed before the parties to negotiate an agreement.

82. B. An arbitrator is a neutral third party to whom disputing parties submit their differences for a decision. A permanent arbitrator resolves conflicts for the life of the contract.

83. A. Constructive discharge occurs when employees claim their working conditions were so intolerable that they were forced to quit. The examples above could lead to a constructive discharge claim.

84. **D.** *The Worker Adjustment and Retraining Notification (WARN) Act requires a 60 calendar notice to be given to employees in the event of mass layoffs or plant closings. The Act does not prevent employees from being fired.*

85. **B.** *Transactional leadership offer a reward for achieved goals. Coaches work with employees to develop skills so they can function independently. Quid pro quo means this for that, a term relevant in sexual harassment cases.*

86. **C.** *Leapfrogging (also known as parallel, pattern bargaining or whipsawing) is a bargaining strategy where the union negotiates with one employer at a time and uses the gains made as a base for negotiating with the next employer.*

87. **C.** *The Employee Retirement Income Security Act or ERISA is a Federal law that sets standards of protection for individuals in most voluntarily established, private-sector retirement plans with minimum standard requirements.*

88. **C.** *The Family Medical Leave Act (FMLA) allows for unforeseeable leave in which case the employee is to notify the employer of the absence as soon as they can.*

89. **A.** *The Labor Management Relations Act also known as the Taft-Hartley Act was passed in 1947. The Act prohibited closed shops, allowed states to enact right-to-work laws and created the Federal Mediation and Conciliation Service (FMCS) to assist in the settlement of labor disputes.*

90. **D.** *Alternative dispute resolution forms are methods used to solve disagreements without litigation.*

91. **C.** *Open communication from the top-bottom and from bottom-up can help ensure a work environment that does not require employee representatives or unions.*

92. **A.** *The Office of Labor Management Standards of the DOL administers and enforces most provisions of the Labor-Management Reporting and Disclosure Act of 1959 (LMRDA).*

93. **C.** *When employees are brought together to research or recommend a solution for a specific mission, this group is called a task force.*

94. **B.** *Negative correlation is a relationship between two variables in which one variable increases as the other decreases, and vice versa.*

95. **B.** *The classification method of job evaluation identifies and uses key benchmark positions to determine the worth of a job. It consists of the Point Factor and Hay system.*

96. **B.** *Wage compression is a form of pay inequity where new employees are paid wages higher than those being paid to the current employees. This can happen when a particular skillset exceeds the availability or the salary structure does not align with the external market data.*

97. **B.** *Compa-ratio is calculated as* $\frac{\text{Base salary} \times 100}{\text{Midpoint of salary range}}$

98. **D.** *A positive correlation is a relationship between two variables where if one variable increases, the other one also increases; also if one variable decreases, the other decreases.*

99. A. *The cost/benefit analysis compares the costs of a proposed project to benefits that will be realized.*

100. B. *Flex-time is an alternative work schedule where employees can work flexible hours to enable them attend to personal business.*

Section 2 Questions

101. A Summary Plan Description, Annual Reports and Participant Benefit Rights Reports are reporting requirements of which of the following laws?
a. Title VII of the Civil Rights Act.
b. ERISA.
c. COBRA.
d. HIPAA.

102. The CHEQ organisation makes corporate decisions based on feedback from a group of experts who anonymously reply to questionnaires to arrive at a consensus. This is known as?
a. Delphi technique.
b. Facilitation.
c. Committee analysis.
d. Judgement forecasts.

103. An account that allows employees to set aside pre-tax money to pay for qualified medical and childcare costs is called?
a. Health funds.
b. Flexible Spending Account.
c. Cafeteria plans.
d. None of the above.

104. The following are tactical accountability measures except?
a. Grievance rates.
b. Cost per hire.
c. Turnover and retention.
d. Return on Investment.

105. The Act that protects health insurance coverage for workers and their families when they change or lose their jobs and establishes national standards to protect individuals' medical records and other personal health information is called?
a. ERISA.
b. HIPAA.
c. COBRA.

d. EEOC.

106. The federal law passed by Congress in 1986 that provides continuing coverage of group health benefits to employees and their families upon the occurrence of certain qualifying events where such coverage would otherwise be terminated is called?
a. OBRA.
b. COBRA.
c. CCPA.
d. FAFSA.

107. Which of the following Acts was designed to improve workforce quality, enhance national productivity and reduce reliance on welfare?
a. Trade Adjustment Assistance.
b. Workforce Investment Act.
c. Unemployment Insurance.
d. RIF Act.

108. When employees own non-forfeitable employer contributions to their pension plans, this is known as?
a. Vesting.
b. Qualified plan.
c. Nonqualified plan.
d. Rabbi trusts.

109. Which of the following acts allowed for catch-up contributions to the retirement plan of employees 50 years or older?
a. Pension Protection Act.
b. Economic Growth and Tax Relief Reconciliation Act.
c. Omnibus Budget Reconciliation Act.
d. Compensation Amendments.

110. The following are examples of non-qualified plans except:
a. Rabbi trusts.
b. Excess deferral plans.
c. Split dollar life-insurance.
d. Target Benefit plan.

111. The GREEN organisation has had a high level of attrition in the HR department. Exit interviews have shown that employees have lost confidence in their supervisors. Which employee engagement approach would best give accurate employee feedback?
a. Newsletters.
b. Skip-level interviews.
c. Brown-bag lunches.
d. Open door policy.

112. The following are voluntary deductions except?
a. 401(k) contributions.
b. Health benefit contributions.
c. Wage garnishments.
d. Union dues.

113. Unregistered shares of ownership in a corporation that are issued to executives, are non-transferable and have a vesting schedule are called?
a. Cafeteria plan.
b. Medical insurance plan.
c. Restricted stock.
d. All of the above.

114. According to Kurt Lewin's change process theory, which of the following are the three stages of change?
a. Unfreezing, Moving, Freezing.
b. Freezing, Melting, Refreezing.
c. Unfreezing, Moving, Refreezing.
d. Moving, Melting, Refreezing.

115. A group of people with common work interests who interact to enhance the group's skills, productivity and expertise is most likely called?
a. Communities of practice.
b. Communities of interest.
c. Knowledge management.
d. Skill transfer.

116. The federal law intended to ensure that persons who serve or have served in the Armed Forces, Reserves, National Guard or other uniformed services are not disadvantaged in their civilian careers because of their service and are promptly reemployed in their civilian jobs upon their return from duty is called?
a. USERRA.
b. VEVRAA.
c. ADEA.
d. EEOC.

117. Methods or practices that have been demonstrated to produce desired results over a period of time are called?
a. Expertise.
b. Best procedure.
c. Standard practice.
d. Best-practice standards.

118. A plan where enrollees are required to choose a primary care physician (PCP) from within the health care network and the PCP may make referrals outside the network for which the employee must submit reimbursement claims is called?
a. Point of Service Plan.
b. Health Maintenance Organization.
c. Preferred Provider Organization.
d. Fee for Service Plan.

119. Amebo is working on a test whereby she compares the mean of the salary deferrals of Nonhighly compensated employees (NHCEs) to that of Highly compensated employees (HCEs). She has to determine the percentage of compensation that has been deferred to the 401(k) plan for the NHCEs and the HCEs; then average the deferral percentages of the NCHEs and the HCEs. For Amebo's firm to pass the test, the ADP of the HCE group may not exceed the ADP for the NHCE group by the lesser of 2 percentage points. What test is Amebo working on?
a. IRS non-discrimination test.
b. Disparate deferral test.
c. Actual deferral percentage test.
d. Excess deferral percentage test.

120. Tim's retirement plan is set up to pay him a specific benefit at retirement. Dayo's retirement plan does not promise a specific benefit at retirement but his employer matches his contributions on a regular basis. What type of retirement plan do Tim and Dayo have?
a. HMO and benefit plan.
b. Defined benefit and Defined contribution plan.
c. Defined contribution and Defined benefit plan.
d. Both have defined benefit retirement plans.

121. Employers with 50 or more full-time employees are required to provide health coverage to full-time employees or pay a tax penalty. Is this statement accurate?
a. No, no law requires that employers provide health coverage for employees.
b. Yes, the EEOC provides that employers provide employees with health coverage.
c. Yes, the PPACA states that employers provide employees with health coverage.

d. No, only veterans are entitled to health coverage.

122. As HR Manager, you're concerned about employee tardiness and you want to make changes to help minimize it. Which of the following will help senior management understand the impact tardiness has on productivity?
a. Gantt chart.
b. Scatter diagram.
c. Recognition diagram.
d. All of the above.

123. Works-for-hire, according to the Copyright Act of 1976, are protected for ------ from the first year of publication or -----years from the year of creation?
a. 95 years, 120 years.
b. 70 years, 120 years.
c. 95 years, 100 years.
d. 50 years, 70 years.

124. Your company will be training entry-level staff with a heavy reliance on their ability to listen as presentations, manuals and handouts will be provided. Also, the employees will be required to take notes often and face the front of the room. Which seating configuration will work best for this?
a. Conference style seating
b. Round tables.
c. Classroom style seating.
d. Theater style seating.

125. The GEEK company is in the process of applying a management model that aims to improve performance of the organization by clearly defining objectives that are agreed to by both management and employees. This approach is an example of;
a. Goal setting.
b. Factual direction.
c. Management by objectives.
d. Performance focus.

126. The Benin organisation intends to develop and implement a tool to help HR and Line Managers identify staffing needs by categorizing current employees. This tool is most likely called?
a. Succession planning.
b. Internal promotion.
c. Replacement chart.
d. Redundancy chart.

127. Your company CEO has decided that HR is to implement new processes which are designed to attract, develop, motivate, and retain productive employees. He

believes this will help meet the company's business goals. This is an example of what kind of program?
a. Performance management.
b. Talent management.
c. Employee relations.
d. Labour development.

128. The **ADDIE** represents a descriptive framework for building effective training and instructional design in five phases. Which of the following is not one of the five phases?
a. Analysis
b. Development.
c. Design.
d. Empowerment.

129. As an HR professional, which of the following is the first step in a change initiative?
a. Engaging Employees.
b. Overcoming Resistance.
c. Communicating change.
d. Reinforce the change.

130. Mandy, a manager in the PROVERBS 31 organisation is known to stimulate and inspire employees to both achieve extraordinary outcomes and develop their own leadership capacity. Mandy's leadership style is called?
a. Transactional.
b. Transformational.
c. Controlling.
d. Laissez-faire.

131. Which of the following is the study of how adults learn?
a. Visual learning.
b. Aged learning.
c. Andragogy.
d. Kinesiology.

132. Which of the following is NOT correct about coaching?
a. It is task-oriented.
b. It is for a short-term.
c. It is the same as counselling.
d. It is performance-driven.

133. A performance management trainer asks the participants to evaluate the training right after the training. The evaluation has questions which ask if the training was a valuable experience and the trainees' perception about the instructor, the topic, the material, its presentation, and the venue. This evaluation type is called:
a. Behavior.
b. Analysis.
c. Learning.
d. Reaction.

134. Which of the following jobs is suitable for telecommuting?
a. Facilities manager.
b. Data entry clerk.
c. Receptionist.
d. All of the above.

135. The Best Belly food-chain company just had a hygiene training. To evaluate how well the training was applied, the HR team is using surveys and interviews to analysis how the training has changed behavior based on the training received. This analysis is what type of evaluation?
a. Assimilation.
b. Behavior.
c. Results.
d. Reaction.

136. The CEO of GRACE company has requested for a change in the performance feedback review process. From the 3rd quarter, the new feedback review must provide a well-rounded and balanced view of employee skills and behaviors. The feedback should also be from a variety of people in the organization and not just the employee's supervisor. This is most likely called?
a. Rating scale.
b. Cross-functional review.
c. 360-degree feedback.
d. Qualified review.

137. A Summary Plan Description (SPD) which has had changes must be prepared and distributed how often to participants?
a. 10 years.
b. 7 years.
c. 5 years.
d. 12 years.

138. A learning curve that involves rapid increases in learning at the beginning which then diminishes as the employee becomes more familiar is called?
a. Negatively accelerating learning curve.
b. Investment accelerating curve.
c. Plateau learning curve.
d. S-shaped learning curve.

139. Which of the following is not protected by the Copyright Act of 1976?
a. Works by children below 18 years.
b. Works by the U.S. government.
c. Musical works.
d. Pantomimes.

140. The managers at SEGI use a method of performance appraisal which involves identifying and describing specific events where the employee did something really well or something that needs improvement. This performance appraisal is called:
a. 360-degree feedback.
b. Behavioral incidents.
c. Critical incidents.
d. Performance tracking.

141. The CEO of your fitness company wants to train the trainers in muscle development techniques. He believes most trainers learn best by watching the technique images. This is an example of which learning style?
a. Auditory.
b. Visual.
c. Kinesthetic.
d. Eyeballing.

142. Ann recently told her boss that the information she used for her presentation is in the public domain, what does Ann mean?
a. The information Ann used is protected by copyright.
b. The information Ann used is in the fair use doctrine.
c. The information Ann used is past the author's lifetime plus 70 years.
d. The information Ann used is a work for hire.

143. What type of legal protection applies only to the ornamental appearance of an item?
a. Plant patent.
b. Utility patent.
c. Design patent.
d. Ornamental patent.

144. Plant patents are protected for how long?
a. 14 years.
b. 20 years.
c. 7 years.
d. 21 years.

145. Which of the following is not correct with regard to DMAIC under Six Sigma?
a. Competence.
b. Define.
c. Measure.
d. Analyze.

146. The Uniformed Services Employment and Reemployment Rights Act (USERRA) protects a uniformed service member's reemployment rights except?
a. The employee has worked for 30 days.
b. The uniformed service member is an independent contractor.
c. The employee is a key employee as defined under the FMLA.
d. All uniformed service members are protected by USERRA.

147. The National Labor Relations Act applies to which of the following?
a. State government.
b. Employers involved in interstate railroads and airlines.
c. Private universities.
d. Employers of only agricultural workers.

148. A plan which develops alternatives to recover and protect a business' operations when property, information systems or people have been disrupted is called?
a. Emergency response plan.
b. Disaster recovery plan.
c. Continuity plans.
d. Competence plans.

149. If an injured employee is willing and able to perform some but not all of the key duties of his job which is reasonable and approved, which of the following return-to-work programs applies?
a. Alternate profession.
b. Independent medical exam.
c. Modified duty.
d. Reasonable accommodation.

150. Which of the following is an illegal strike?
a. Economic strike.
b. Unfair Labor Practice Strike.
c. Recognition strike.
d. Sit-down strike.

151. Ajaw Inc. requires its temporary workers to handle chemicals as an essential function. According to the Hazard Communication Standard, which of the following is accurate?
a. The chemical company is responsible for providing complete Hazard Communication compliance training for the temporary workers.
b. The temporary workers' staffing agency provides complete training to the temporary workers.
c. The staffing agency will provide generic hazard training and information concerning categories of chemicals while the chemical company is responsible for providing site-specific hazard training.
d. The temporary worker must be licensed in the hazards they will be exposed to.

152. A health plan administrator whose computer was hacked into should be concerned about which of the following laws?
a. Health Insurance Portability & Accountability Act.
b. Consolidated Omnibus Budget Reconciliation Act.
c. Workers Adjustment and Retraining Act.
d. Employee Retirement Income Security Act.

153. OSHA requires which of the following for compliance with its blood-borne pathogens standard?

a. Written exposure control plan that details preventive steps against the spread of blood-borne pathogens.
b. Use of personal protective equipment for all employees.
c. Safety training for all employees.
d. All of the above.

154. Hot cargo clauses were made illegal by which of the following?
a. The Wagner Act.
b. The Labor Management Relations Act.
c. The Clayton Act.
d. The Norris-La Guardia Act.

155. The TEN company has been found guilty of willful violation of health and safety standards, the company can be fined up to _____ per violation?
a. $10,000.
b. $0.
c. $70,000.
d. $100,000.

156. The legislation enacted to promote the accuracy, fairness, and privacy of consumer information contained in the files of consumer reporting agencies is called?
a. Fair Credit Reporting Act of 1970.
b. Title VII of 1964.
c. Affordable Care Act.
d. Disclosure Act.

157. For an injury to be recordable, it must be work-related. Which of the following is a work-related injury?
a. Colds or flu.
b. Injuries from choking on a grape at lunch.
c. Shaving cuts in the employer's bathroom.
d. A brick falls on an engineer at a construction site.

158. Which act protects investors from the possibility of fraudulent accounting activities, mandates strict reforms to improve financial disclosures from corporations and prevents accounting fraud?
a. WARN Act.
b. Fair Credit Reporting Act.
c. Sarbanes-Oxley Act.
d. ERISA.

159. Which of the following is not a relevant question in the strategic planning process?
a. Where are we now?
b. Who are our competitors?
c. Where do we want to be?
d. How will we know when we arrive?

160. An aspirational description of what an organization would like to achieve or accomplish in the mid-term or long-term is called?
a. Mission statement.
b. Vision statement.
c. Business plan.
d. Business process.

161. Jimi became injured on his job and believes he has developed an illness that is related to his work. Which of the following can Jimi claim?
a. Retaliation.
b. Worker's Injury claim.
c. Workers' compensation.
d. Ergonomic disability.

162. The Managing Director recently approved a statement of purpose for the YES company which details its reason for existing. The statement will guide the actions of the organization, spell out its overall goal and guide decision-making. This is known as?
a. Organizational guide.
b. Vision statement.
c. Mission statement.
d. Statement of purpose.

163. The final question in the strategic planning process is?
a. How will we know when we get there?
b. Where do we want to be?
c. What's our mission?
d. How will we get there?

164. When a manager chooses to exempt an employee from a difficult test for having perfect attendance, what concept of operant conditioning is this?
a. Negative reinforcement.
b. Positive reinforcement.
c. Punishment.
d. Extinction.

165. Bini believes in a style of management that assumes that employees are naturally unmotivated and dislike working. He states that management must actively intervene to get things done. This style of management is called?
a. Negative management.
b. ULP management.
c. Theory X management.
d. Theory Y management.

166. Employer-provided group term life insurance that exceeds $50,000 for an employee is subject to which of the following?
a. The provisions of OBRA.
b. Tax deductions on the value of the imputed income.

c. Sarbanes-Oxley provisions.
d. None of the above.

167. Appia has asked for a union representative to be present at an employer-organized investigation. Which of the following is NOT one of the options her employer has with regard to Ann's request?
a. Continue the investigation if evidence against Appia is job-related.
b. Discontinue the interview until the union representative arrives.
c. Decide not to conduct the interview at all.
d. Give Appia the choice of voluntarily waiving the Weingarten rights.

168. Which of the following is NOT an example of an alternative dispute resolution?
a. Arbitration.
b. Mediation.
c. Litigation.
d. Constructive confrontation.

169. The three OSHA forms; OSHA form 300 (log of work-related injuries and illnesses), OSHA form 300A (summary of work-related injuries and illnesses) and OSHA form 301 (injury and illness incident report) must be retained for how long?
a. 5 years.
b. 3 years.
c. 7 years.
d. 1 year.

170. Dami, a Compliance Safety and Health Officer (CSHO), has been sent to conduct an inspection of the YEP construction company. However, the HR manager of YEP company refuses Dami entry because Dami gave the company no notice. Is Dami required to give notice before an OSHA inspection?
a. Yes, it is due process.
b. No, the CSHO is not required to give the company notice before an inspection.
c. No, Dami is protected by Title VII.
d. Yes, all inspections require 15 days notice.

171. When OSHA conducts planned inspections of industries that have a high incident rate for death and injury, this is called?
a. Follow-up inspections.
b. Compulsory inspections.
c. Programmed inspections.
d. Fatality inspections.

172. A notice of contest is to be filed by an employer who wishes to contest an OSHA citation or proposed penalty. This should be filed in how many days?
a. 10 days.
b. 15 days.
c. 7 days.

d. 5 days.

173. When FMLA leave is foreseeable, an employee is to give the employer ---- days notice and the employer is required to give the employee ----- days to submit medical certification to support a FMLA request;
a. 20 days; 15 days.
b. 30 days; 10 days.
c. 20 days; 7 days.
d. 30 days; 15 days.

174. Picketing which occurs where the targeted primary employer's work site is also the work site of a neutral employer is called?
a. Recognitional picketing.
b. Consumer picketing.
c. Hot-cargo picketing.
d. Common situs picketing.

175. An election bar where a union withdraws an election petition which results in an election bar for 6 months is called?
a. Contract Bar.
b. Prior Petition Bar.
c. Blocking charge Bar.
d. Withdrawn Petition Bar.

176. Robert Stakes said, "When the cook tastes the soup, that's formative. When the guests taste the soup, that's summative." What does this mean?
a. Formative evaluation tests the training content prior to delivery while summative evaluation occurs post-delivery of the training.
b. Formative evaluation evaluates the trainer while summative evaluation evaluates the trainees.
c. Formative evaluation evaluates the trainee's reaction while the summative evaluation evaluates the training effect on the bottom-line.
d. Formative and summative evaluation have the major difference of the degree of transfer of training.

177. When your company is the primary employer but has a co-employment arrangement with an organisation who handles specific employer functions such as payroll, benefits, tax remittance and related government filings, the secondary organisation is most likely;
a. Independent contractor.
b. Professional Employer Organization.
c. Outsourcing company.
d. Payroll company.

178. Which of the following competences is critical for an HR professional to have?
a. Conflict resolution skills.
b. Litigation.
c. Business knowledge.
d. Recruiting acumen.

179. Ade intends to apply for FMLA leave to care for his son who is a service member with a serious injury sustained while on active duty. How many weeks of FMLA leave is Ade entitled to?
a. 12 weeks.
b. 26 weeks.
c. 12 weeks plus an additional 11 weeks.
d. 12 weeks of paid leave.

Use the table below to answer question 179 -183.

GROUP	APPLICANTS	HIRED	SELECTION RATE
BLUES	100	35	
BLACKS	122	12	
WHITES	170	20	
YELLOWS	440	35	
TOTAL			

180. The table above is most likely used to calculate which of the following?
a. Applicant tracking.
b. Disparate treatment.
c. Affirmative action.
d. Adverse impact.

181. What is the selection rate for the blues and the blacks?
a. 35% and 10%.
b. 25% and 12%
c. 45% and 9%.
d. 15% and 35%.

182. Which group has the highest selection rate?
a. Yellows.
b. Blues.
c. Blacks.
d. Whites.

183. In which of these groups did disparate impact NOT occur?
a. Black.
b. White.
c. Yellow.
d. None of the above.

184. What type of leadership is most effective where decisions are nonroutine and do not need to be made rapidly?
a. Transformational.
b. Laissez-faire.
c. Participative.
d. Transactional.

185. Which of the following health insurance plans will a make contract arrangement directly with an employer?
a. Exclusive Provider Organization.
b. Fee For Service Plan.
c. Physician Hospital Organization.
d. Preferred Provider Organization.

186. What type of learning curve will be applicable to a production line?
a. Negatively accelerating learning curve.
b. Positively accelerating learning curve.
c. S-shaped learning curve.
d. Plateau learning curve.

187. The Obiageli company uses the paired comparison method of performance appraisal for the Engineering department. If there are 10 full-time engineers and 2 consultant engineers, with how many engineers will each engineer be compared with?
a. 10.
b. 11.
c. 9.
d. 12.

188. What law allowed for jury trials where the plaintiff seeks compensatory or punitive damages?
a. Civil Rights Act of 1991.
b. Civil Rights Act of 1964.
c. Title VII of 1991
d. Equal Employment Opportunity Act of 1972.

189. The relationship between results and the resources required to produce them is the basis for?
a. Resource allocation.
b. Cost-benefit analysis.
c. Budgetary analysis.
d. Training needs analysis.

190. A type of interviewer bias in which the interviewer allows one strong point that works against the candidate to overshadow all other information is called?
a. Horn effect.
b. Halo effect.
c. Similar-to-me.
d. Knowledge of predictor bias.

191. In transforming the focus of an organization from product to customer, the HR director's primary role is to ensure that:
a. Employees agree on change management principles and processes.
b. Employees are given training in change process techniques of unfreezing, moving and refreezing.
c. Employee communications, training, performance reviews, and rewards are properly aligned.
d. All of the above.

192. Responses of an interview candidate that are socially acceptable rather than factual is called?
a. Cultural noise.
b. Racial bias.
c. Poor listening skills.
d. Central tendency.

193. The legal doctrine under which a party can be held liable for the wrongful actions of another party is called?
a. Constructive discharge.
b. Employer responsibility.
c. Vicarious liability.
d. Quid pro quo.

194. To achieve maximum impact, an organization's ethics training program should:
a. Include the organization's executive management.
b. Refer to items from the organization's code of conduct policy.
c. Focus on legal applications of ethics.
d. Teach employees the consequences of corporate scandal.

195. Which court case stated that items used to validate employment requirements must be job-related and subjective supervisor rankings are not sufficient for validation?
a. Washington v. Davis.
b. City of Richmond v. J.A. Croson Company.
c. Albemarle v. Moody.
d. Taxman v. Board of Education of Piscataway.

196. Which of the following is not one of the four key areas of the balanced scorecard developed by Robert Kaplan and David Norton?
a. Financial results.
b. Customer results.
c. Internal business processes.
d. Competence measurement.

197. During an interview, questions related to a disabled applicant's potential performance on the job may include all of the following except:
a. "Do you have legal authorization to work in the USA?"
b. "How would you perform the essential tasks of the job for which you have applied?"

c. "Do you have any physical or other limitations?"
d. "Would you describe your attendance on your last job?"

198. A financial statement that summarizes a company's assets, liabilities and shareholders' equity at a specific point in time is called?
a. Cash flow statement
b. Balance sheet.
c. Budget.
d. Income statement.

199. The first step in recruiting for a newly vacated position is to determine the:
a. Budget available for recruitment.
b. Establish the position's compensation.
c. Post a job ad for candidates.
d. Need for changes to the job description.

200. Which of the following protected class can never be a Bona Fide Occupational Qualification (BFOQ)?
a. Gender.
b. Race.
c. National origin.
d. Religion.

Section 2 Answers and Explanations

101. B. *The Employee Retirement Income Security Act (ERISA) of 1974 has the reporting requirements of a summary plan description, annual reports and participant benefit rights reports.*

102. A. *The Delphi technique obtains input from experts anonymously till a consensus is arrived at.*

103. B. *Flexible Spending Accounts allow employees to set aside non-taxable funds to pay for medical expenses.*

104. D. *Return on Investment is a business impact measure. A tactical accountability measure evaluates the effectiveness of specific HR programs.*

105. B. *The Health Insurance Portability and Accountability Act (HIPAA) protects health insurance coverage for employees when they change or lose jobs and sets standards to keep protected health information (PHI) private and confidential.*

106. B. *COBRA, the Consolidated Omnibus Budget Reconciliation Act, provides continuing coverage of health benefits to employees and dependents when qualifying events occur for a certain period of time, usually 18 months. For disability cases, length of coverage is 29 months. For employee death, divorce or loss of dependent status, length of coverage is 36 months.*

107. B. *The Workforce Investment Act helps with job training programs to improve worker skills.*

108. A. *Vesting is the process by which an employee accrues non-forfeitable rights over employer-provided stock incentives or employer contributions made to the employee's qualified retirement plan account or pension plan. Employees are always 100% vested in their own contributions.*

109. B. *The Economic Growth and Tax Relief Reconciliation Act increased contribution limits and allowed for catch-up contributions for employees 50 years or older.*

110. D. *A nonqualified plan is any type of tax-deferred, employer-sponsored retirement plan that falls outside of Employee Retirement Income Security Act (ERISA) guidelines. A target benefit plan is a qualified plan.*

111. B. *The skip-level interview is an employee engagement approach in which employees are interviewed by their manager's manager to to provide accurate insight on job satisfaction or the lack thereof.*

112. C. *Wage garnishments are statutory deductions from an employee's pay to satisfy a debt. It is an involuntary deduction.*

113. C. *Restricted stock refers to the stock of a company offered to executives, this is not fully transferable until certain conditions (restrictions) have been met.*

114. C. *Kurt Lewin's change process theory has three stages of change; Unfreezing, Moving and Refreezing.*

115. A. *A community of practice is a group of people who share a concern or a passion for something they do, and learn how to do it better as they interact regularly. It is effective in learning and knowledge management.*

116. A. *The Uniformed Services Employment and Reemployment Rights Act (USERRA) ensures reemployment for military individuals upon return from duty. Virtually all U.S. employers must comply with USERRA. VEVRAA (Vietnam Era Veterans' Readjustment Assistance Act) is a federal law which prohibits discrimination against veterans by requiring federal contractors to list all job openings with state employment agencies except senior-level management positions, positions filled from within and positions lasting 3 days or less.*

117. D. *A best practice is a technique or methodology that, through experience and research, has been proven to reliably lead to a desired result.*

118. A. *Point of Service plan is a managed care health insurance plan which has network physicians and also allows for referrals outside the network.* **Important-understand the different health plans**

119. C. *The Actual Deferral Percentage (ADP) test is to ensure no discrimination between HCEs and Non-HCEs. The test compares the average (same as mean) salary deferral, as a percentage of pre-tax compensation of highly compensated employees (HCE) to that of non-highly compensated employees (NHCE). To pass the test, the ADP of the HCE may not exceed the ADP of the NHCE by a factor of 1.25 or 2 percentage points.*

120. B. *A defined benefit plan provides a specific benefit upon retirement (Tim) while for a defined contribution plan, the contributions to the plan are known but the end benefit at retirement is not known.*

121. C. *The Patient Protection and Affordable Care Act (PPACA) also called Obamacare provides that employers with 50 or more full time equivalent (FTE) employees are required to provide health coverage to full-time employees or pay a tax penalty.*

122. B. *The scatter diagram provides a visual representation of the relationship between two variables; it lets you see the patterns in data and confirm or negate assumptions.*

123. A. *Works for hire are protected for the shorter of 95 years from the first year of publication or 120 years from the year of creation, whichever expires first.*

124. C. *In classroom style seating, rectangular tables are arranged in horizontal rows so that participants are facing the front of the room. Classroom style is used when participants will need to write or refer to handouts during the meeting.*

125. C. *Management by Objectives (MBO) is the process of defining specific objectives within an organization that management can convey to employees and decide on how to achieve each objective.*

126. C. *A replacement chart lists the critical job roles in a company, the employees currently positioned in those roles, their competencies, the current vacancies and potential replacement for the vacancies. Employees are categorized into Ready for promotion, Develop for future promotion, Satisfactory in current position and Replace.*

127. B. *Talent management strategies focus on five primary areas: attracting, selecting, engaging, developing and retaining employees to gain competitive advantage and achieve business goals.*

128. D. *The ADDIE has 5 elements which are Analysis, Design, Development, Implementation, and Evaluation.*

129. B. *The first step will be overcoming resistance by helping employees understand the need for change, the rationale behind the decisions for change and creating an urgency for change.*

130. B. *Transformational leaders inspire and motivate employees. Laissez-faire leadership is where all the rights and power to make decisions are fully given to the employees.*

131. C. *Andragogy means adult education.*

132. C. *Coaching is different from counselling. Counselling is assistance and guidance in resolving personal, social, or psychological problems and difficulties. Coaching equips employees with tools and knowledge to fully develop their potentials.*

133. D. *The reaction evaluation type helps to understand how well the training was received by your audience following a training event or course. It solicits opinions of the learning experience.*

134. B. *Telecommuting is the way of accomplishing work tasks from off-site locations, usually the employee's home, through channels such as telephones and computers. A data entry clerk is suited to telecommuting.*

135. B. *The Behavior evaluation level analyses how training has changed the trainees' behavior. This looks at how trainees apply the information taught.*

136. C. *The 360-degree feedback will include direct feedback from an employee's subordinates, peers, and supervisor, as well as a self-evaluation.*

137. C. *ERISA requires that the SPD which has had changes be prepared and distributed every 5 years. Whether changes have occurred or not, a new SPD must be distributed every 10 years.*

138. A. *A negatively accelerating learning curve has quick increases in learning e.g the task of operating a cash register.*

139. B. Copyright protection is not available for works of the United States Government.

140. C. Critical incident is a performance appraisal method that is used for collecting direct observations of specific events of significance.

141. B. Visual learners learn information most effectively when they see something, for example, pictures, diagrams, films and videos.

142. C. Public domain works are not restricted by copyright, these are all works published in the USA before 1923 and works past the life of the author plus 70 years.

143. C. Design patent is a form of legal protection to protect the way an item looks, it grants this protection to the ornamental design of an item.

144. B. Plant and utility patents are protected for 20 years. Design patents are protected for 14 years.

145. A. The Six Sigma methodology is an acronym called DMAIC which means Define, Measure, Analyze, Improve and Control.

146. B. USERRA does not provide reinstatement protection for temporary employees, independent contractors or employees who have been separated from service with a disqualifying discharge.

147. C. The NLRA applies to most private sector employers, including manufacturers, retailers and private universities. The NLRA does not apply to federal, state, or local governments; employers who employ only agricultural workers; and employers subject to the Railway Labor Act (interstate railroads and airlines).

148. B. A disaster recovery plan is a set of procedures established to recover and protect a business' infrastructure in the event of a disaster.

149. C. Modified duty is an offer for a temporary work assignment made to a worker who is recovering from an illness or injury and who has received clearance from a physician to return to work under specific limitations.

150. D. A sit-down strike occurs when workers occupy and sit in their place of employment and refuse to work or allow others to work until the strike is settled. Economic strikes are based on disputes over wages and benefits; Unfair Labor Practice (ULP) strikes are to protest employer illegal activity; Recognition strikes are intended to force employers to recognize unions. ULP strikers cannot be permanently replaced but economic strikers can be.

151. C. In meeting the requirements of OSHA's Hazard Communication Standard, the temporary agency employer would provide generic hazard training and information concerning the categories of chemicals employees may potentially encounter while the host employer is responsible for providing site-specific hazard training.

152. A. HIPAA requires the protection and confidential handling of protected health information (PHI).

153. A. For blood-borne pathogens, OSHA requires a written exposure control plan that informs employees of preventive steps, post-exposure evaluation and incident evaluation procedures.

154. B. Hot cargo clauses were made illegal by the Taft-Hartley Act which is also called the Labor Management Relations Act.

155. **C.** According to OSHA, willful violations range from $5,000 to $70,000 per violation.

156. **A.** The Fair Credit Reporting Act regulates how consumer reporting agencies use consumer reports to ensure accuracy and privacy.

157. **D.** Injuries are not work-related if it occurs to the general public, certain parking lot accidents, non-work-induced mental illnesses, colds or flu, injuries from personal meals/grooming, self-inflicted injuries or natural disasters.

158. **C.** The Sarbanes-Oxley Act was passed to protect shareholders and the general public from accounting errors and fraudulent practices of corporations as well as improve the accuracy of corporate disclosures.

159. **B.** The strategic planning process has 4 main questions: where are we now?; where do we want to be?; how will we get there?; how will we know when we arrive?

160. **B.** A vision statement describes where a business is headed and what it will look like when it's gets there.

161. **C.** Workers' compensation is a form of insurance providing wage replacement and medical benefits to employees injured or who fall ill in the course of employment in exchange for relinquishing the right to sue the employer for negligence.

162. **C.** A mission statement defines the company's goals, ethics, culture, and standard for decision-making.

163. **A.** The final step in the strategic planning process is the strategy evaluation phase which should answer the question, "How will we know when we get there?"

164. **A.** Negative reinforcement encourages an acceptable behavior by taking away something unpleasant. Positive reinforcement encourages the behavior by providing a pleasant reward. Punishment is designed to weaken or eliminate a response rather than increase it.

165. **C.** Douglas MacGregor of MIT expounded The X and Y Theory. Theory X managers believe that workers are naturally unmotivated and dislike working while Theory Y managers assume that workers are happy to work, self-motivated and creative.

166. **B.** When employer-provided group term life insurance exceeds $50,000 for an employee, the value of the excess coverage (imputed income *understand what this means*) must be reported as income and is subject to Social Security and Medicare taxes.

167. **A.** The three options the employer has are options B, C and D. Option D could mean giving the employee the choice of having the interview without representation or ending the interview. The employer does not have the option of continuing the investigation except the employee voluntarily waives the Weingarten rights.

168. **C.** Alternative dispute resolution refers to any method used to resolve a dispute between parties without resorting to litigation.

169. **A.** The OSHA forms must be retained for 5 years following the end of the calendar year they cover.

170. **B.** OSHA inspections can be conducted by a CSHO without notice to the organisation.

171. C. A programmed inspection is scheduled due to a selection criteria by OSHA. This criteria may be injury rates, death rates, exposure to toxic substances or a high amount of lost workdays for the industry type.

172. B. An employer can contest an OSHA citation for violations by filing a notice of contest. This should be filed within 15 working days.

173. D. When the need for FMLA leave is foreseeable, an employee must give the employer at least 30 days notice. Employers must provide at least 15 calendar days for an employee to submit a medical certification to support a FMLA request.

174. D. Common-situs picketing is an illegal picketing by union workers due to a grievance against a single employer at a worksite which is shared with other employers. Hot-cargo agreements are agreements between an employer and a union where the employer agrees to not undertake any work coming from another employer whom the union has a dispute with.

175. B. The NLRB will not hold an election where there is an election bar. The prior petition bar is in place when the union withdraws a petition for an election prior to the election, this results into an election bar for 6 months.

176. A. A formative evaluation is used to test the training design/process before the training is delivered to the training participants. A summative evaluation evaluates the outcome of a training. Summative evaluation has 4 levels; Reaction, Learning, Behavior and Results.

177. B. A professional employer organization works with a primary employer to provide payroll, benefits and human resource services through a business-to-business relationship called co-employment.

178. C. An HR executive must understand how the organization operates in the business context. This includes understanding key business terms and measures towards the achievement of company goals.

179. B. FMLA allows for 26 weeks of unpaid leave to care for a family member who is a covered service member with a serious injury or illness sustained while on active duty. Other cases for which the FMLA leave can be taken is for 12 weeks. FMLA is generally unpaid leave.

180. D. An adverse impact occurs when the selection rate for a protected class is less than 4/5ths or 80% of the selection rate of the group with the largest selection rate. The table above is used to calculate adverse impact.

181. A. The selection rate is calculated by dividing the number of hires by the number of applicants for each group. The blues' rate is 35/100=35% and the blacks' rates is 12/122=10% appr.

182. B. The group of blues has a selection rate of 35%, the blacks 10%, the whites 12% and the yellows 8%. The blues have the highest selection rate of 35%.

183. D. The 4/5th or 80% of the group with the highest selection rate is 28% which is 80% of 35, the selection rate for the blues. All other groups have selection rates lower than 28%. Therefore, disparate impact occurred for every other group.

184. C. A participative or democratic leadership style is ideal when decisions do not need to be made instantly and in which the input of others will lead to a better result.

185. C. Physician Hospital Organization (PHO) is a legal entity generally formed by physicians and hospitals with the intention of negotiating contracts with employer organizations to provide services.

186.   A. A production line or an assembly line consists of workers who do a succession of routine tasks. These tasks usually follow a Negatively accelerating learning curve.

187.   C. The paired comparison method of performance appraisal compares each employee with every other employee in a group. Consultants not employees so they will not be included in the appraisal. Each engineer will be compared with the other 9 engineers.

188.   A. The Civil Rights Act of 1991 provides that any party in a civil suit in which punitive or compensatory damages are sought may demand a jury trial.

189.   B. Cost-benefit analysis focuses on the relationship between results (the benefits) and resources required (the costs).

190.   A. The horn effect is a tendency to allow one's judgement of another person, especially in a job interview, to be unduly influenced by an unfavourable (horns) first impression. The halo effect is the opposite, i.e. a favourable (halo) first impression.

191.   C. HR's primary role in a customer-focused organization is to align employee behavior - training, communications and performance management.

192.   A. Cultural noise occurs when a candidate gives responses that are conventional but not revealing.

193.   C. Vicarious liability occurs when an employer is held liable for the wrongdoings of its employees, provided it can be shown that they took place in the course of their employment.

194.   A. Leadership strongly influences employee behavior. When executives participate in ethics training and model ethical behavior, this reinforces the importance of such behavior organization-wide.

195.   C. The Albemarle Paper v. Moody is a 1975 court ruling that stated that items used to validate employment requirements must be job-related. Washington v. Davis is a court ruling that dealt with job testing and discrimination.

196.   D. The balanced scorecard is a strategic planning and management tool used to align business activities to the vision and strategy of the organization, improve internal and external communications and monitor organization performance against the strategic goals. The four key areas are financial results, customer results, key internal processes and learning/innovation.

197.   C. The Equal Employment Opportunity Commission (EEOC) states that employers cannot ask any questions at the pre-offer stage that are likely to give information about a disability. Employers can ask about an applicant's prior attendance record and can ask a candidate to describe or demonstrate how they would perform a job.

198.   B. A balance sheet shows an organization's assets, liabilities, and equity at a particular point in time, detailing the balance of income and expenditure over the preceding period.

199.   D. A job description should be updated regularly to reflect job changes. This is the first essential step to help recruiters understand the job requirements and recruit effectively.

200.   B. Race and color can never be BFOQs.

Section 3 Questions

201. An engineering startup tests job applicants on their software programming skills. A year later, the organization calculates the correlation between the hired applicants' scores and their performance as employees and found a positive correlation. What does this mean?
a. Changes in programming skills cause changes in job performance.
b. Better-performing employees scored higher on the tests.
c. A variance in programming skills and job performance was identified.
d. A statistical difference exists between the programming training and job performance.

202. Employee bonuses linked to an individual's continued employment with an organization so that key performers have strong incentives to stay with the organization due to significant losses if they were to leave are called?
a. Golden parachute.
b. Vesting.
c. Golden handcuffs.
d. Executive incentives.

203. A company who is active in partnerships with local emergency-response teams and provides disaster relief items when applicable is most likely engaged in?
a. Strategic relationships.
b. Corporate Responsibility.
c. Corporate Governance.
d. Offshoring.

204. Employees working under an F-1 student visa are exempt from:
a. Federal income taxes.
b. State taxes.
c. Social Security taxes.
d. ERISA.

205. Who introduced the Total Quality Management Theory?
a. Joseph Juran.
b. Edwards Deming.
c. Kaoru Ishikawa.
d. Philip Crosby.

206. "A method for assessing aptitude and performance which is applied to a group of participants by trained assessors using various aptitude diagnostic processes in order to obtain information about applicants' abilities or development potential." This is most likely referring to?
a. Assessment center.
b. In-Box test.
c. Cognitive Ability Test.
d. Realistic Job Preview.

207. A manufacturing manager of a 1200-employee, nonunion organization tells the HR professional that there will be a plant closing of approximately 240 employees within the next 2 months. The organization plans to use seniority as a basis for selecting the affected employees and will not provide a severance package. Which law should be of initial concern?
a. NLRA.
b. FLSA.
c. WARN.
d. ADEA.

208. Which of the following statements about the Landrum–Griffin Act is true?
a. It outlawed yellow dog contracts.
b. It was referred to as the labor's bill of rights.
c. It applies to railroad companies and airlines.
d. It placed controls on union operations.

209. Which of the following tests is best suited for testing a candidate's coordination and ability to manually manipulate the body to perform a physical movement?
a. Psychomotor assessment tests.
b. Cognitive ability tests.
c. Aptitude tests.
d. Personality tests.

210. Which of the following steps should be taken first in order to reduce turnover?
a. Conduct exit interviews to determine why employees are leaving.
b. Do a competitor survey to determine their pay structures.
c. Increase employee benefits.
d. Improve background checks.

211. An application form designed to assign numeric values to responses provided by applicants in a bid to give higher scores to areas that have a strong relationship to job performance is called?
a. Job specific employment application.
b. Weighted employment application.
c. Job performance application.
d. Numeric application.

212. The Omnibus Budget Reconciliation Act of 1993 does NOT require which of the following?
a. Group health plans honor qualified medical child support orders.
b. Tax deductions for executive pay be capped at $1 million per year.
c. Income tax be withheld from some distributions to rollover accounts.
d. Group health coverage be offered for children placed for adoption before the adoption is final.

213. A manufacturer has contracts in excess of $50,000 to provide a specific machinery to the U.S. Airforce. It also manufactures recreational vehicles. Under Executive Order 11246, this organization must:

a. Have a written affirmative action plan.
b. Use only U.S. Army-approved suppliers.
c. Use the state job service office for recruitment.
d. Give preferential employment opportunities to veterans for senior roles.

214. The Act which simplified the actual deferral percentage (ADP) tests for 401(k) plans and redefined highly compensated employees for small enterprises is called?
a. Economic Growth and Tax Relief Reconciliation Act.
b. Small Business Job Protection Act.
c. Pension Protection Act.
d. EEOA.

215. Which guideline is most important in creating recruitment advertisements?
a. Encourage applications from the disabled.
b. Avoid exclusionary requirements that are not job related.
c. Include alignment with equal employment opportunity laws.
d. Ensure diversity compliance

216. The Act which lowered age limits for participation and vesting in pension plans is called?
a. COBRA.
b. HIPAA.
c. Retirement Equity Act.
d. Older Worker Benefit Protection Act.

217. An organization receives a resume showing that an applicant is qualified for an available position, but decides not to interview the applicant because of records obtained from a previous employer indicating that the individual has a mental disability. The organization:
a. Has protected itself against charges of negligent hiring.
b. Is in violation of OWBPA regulations.
c. Is in violation of the ADA.
d. Has protected itself against charges of discrimination.

218. A disabled employee has a reduction in hours, under COBRA the employee is eligible for a length of coverage of how many months?
a. 36 months.
b. 2 years.
c. 29 months.
d. 18 months.

219. "Tell me about a situation in which you helped to resolve conflict between subordinates" is an example of what type of interview question?
a. Behavioral.
b. Hypothetical.
c. Situational.
d. Structural.

220. The following are reasons for conducting a needs assessment except?
a. To determine if training is the solution to an identified problem.
b. To determine the cost-benefit analysis of the training.
c. It helps determine the goal of the training.
d. It is a legal requirement for sexual harassment training.

221. What is vicarious liability?
a. When someone is held responsible for the actions or omissions of another person.
b. Expectations of management translated into behaviors and results that employees can deliver.
c. Process of delivering educational or instructional programs to locations away from a classroom.
d. When an employee is responsible for intentional safety lapses in the workplace.

222. Which of the following is an example of indirect compensation?
a. Long-term incentive pay.
b. Social security.
c. Pay differential.
d. Pay for performance.

223. A test is shown to measure a variable believed to be a fundamental trait or characteristic that is important for success in performing the job. What type of validity does the test have?
a. Construct.
b. External.
c. Content.
d. Criterion-related.

224. Tom, an evaluator rates 25 individuals. He places three individuals in the category "outstanding" and three individuals in the category "poor." He places five individuals in the category, "above average" and five more individuals in the category, "below average.", he then places nine individuals in the category, "average". What method of performance appraisal is this?
a. Paired comparison.
b. Forced distribution.
c. Ranking.
d. Forced comparison.

225. Individual presentations and in-baskets are exercises associated with:
a. Assessment centers.
b. Panel interviews.
c. Peer to peer panel.
d. Management ranking.

226. A truck company requires that applicants for a truck driver position take a practical driving test. This is an example of what type of validity?
a. Curricular validity.
b. Construct validity.

c. Content validity.
d. Criterion validity.

227. Which of the following can an organization use to justify a "last hired, first fired" policy?
a. WARN requirements.
b. Job relatedness.
c. Bona fide seniority system.
d. Bona fide occupational qualification.

228. A type of learning curve in which learning occurs in a series of increasing and decreasing returns is called?
a. S-shaped learning curve.
b. Negatively accelerating learning curve.
c. Positively accelerating learning curve.
d. Plateau learning curve.

229. An advantage of cross-training is:
a. Employees will reinforce what they have learnt.
b. Employees become expert in all areas of the department.
c. It encourages teamwork as workers get to know the details of co-workers' jobs.
d. It can be accomplished quickly.

230. Which employee evaluation method is typically thought of as the most valuable for a company?
a. Learning.
b. Results.
c. Formative.
d. Behavior.

231. The technique of behavior modeling has been used most effectively in:
a. Work simplification.
b. Team-building programs.
c. New employee orientation programs.
d. Supervisory skills training programs.

232. Which of the following is the most effective method of evaluating employee performance?
a. Narrative review.
b. Paired comparison.
c. Continuous feedback.
d. Forced review.

233. Which part of training program design is most often overlooked by trainers during the program planning process?
a. Content.
b. Evaluation.
c. Implementation.

d. Participant selection.

234. Dan has trained 30 employees on sexual harassment and put together an evaluation to determine the increase in employee knowledge as a result of the training. This is what type of evaluation?
a. Learning.
b. Reaction.
c. Results.
d. Behavior.

235. Which of the following is not a Bona Fide Occupational Qualification?
a. Mandatory retirement ages for bus drivers and airline pilots.
b. A manufacturer of men's clothing advertises for male models.
c. Lutheran church wants to hire a clerk who is Lutheran.
d. A trendy retail store requires a young Asian lady as a clerk.

236. Which of the following is the best method for ensuring the effectiveness of a training program prior to delivery?
a. Focus group.
b. Delphi technique.
c. Pre-session survey.
d. Pilot program.

237. People who learn best through a hands-on approach are called?
a. Visual learners.
b. Kinesthetic learners.
c. Auditory learners.
d. Read-write learners.

238. Which training strategy is most likely to improve sales employees' effectiveness?
a. Attending a seminar on interaction between sales and customer service.
b. Playing the part of the salesperson who must close the deal in a role-play episode.
c. Attending a carefully researched lecture on closing a sale.
d. Reading and studying the organization's sales handbook.

239. Which of the following refers to the positive expectation and subsequent differential treatment by managers or coworkers that is based on knowledge of valid performance indicators?
a. Primacy effect.
b. Recency effect.
c. Knowledge of predictor.
d. External attribution.

240. To ensure the success of a team-building effort, organizers in HR need to:
a. Reward employees for participation.
b. Indicate to employees that their participation is required.
c. Take pre- and post-measures of the impact of the program.
d. Solicit management's support for the program.

241. Referral bonuses paid for recruitment of new employees are not to be included in the regular rate of pay for overtime considerations when?
a. Participation is strictly voluntary.
b. Recruitment efforts do not involve significant time.
c. The activity is limited to after-hours solicitation as part of the employees' social affairs.
d. When all the conditions of A,B,C are met.

242. Which of the following is not accurate when considering a Behaviorally Anchored Rating Scale (BARS) for an organisation?
a. It requires that each BARS be created from scratch for every position in the company.
b. It requires that the scales be tailored to the nature of the work being performed.
c. It requires a high degree of monitoring and maintenance.
d. It overcomes more rating errors than the graphic rating appraisal method.

243. A planned approach to learning that includes a combination of methods such as classroom, e-learning, self-paced study and performance support is called?
a. Blended learning.
b. CBT Training.
c. Socratic seminar.
d. Vestibule training.

244. Oke worked 60 hours in Week 9 and his pay rate is $13/hour. Oke also receives a bi-weekly productivity bonus of $200. What is Oke's total gross pay for week 9?
a. $910.
b. $1,027.
c. $1,025.
d. $1,102.

245. Which of the following is most important for an employee during the initial period of employment?
a. Pleasant working conditions.
b. Employee handbook.
c. Supervisory feedback.
d. Sympathetic co-workers.

246. Ability of an individual to be sensitive to and understanding of the emotions of others as well as manage his or her own emotions and impulses is called?
a. Emotional Intelligence.
b. Emotions management.
c. Workplace emotions.
d. Professional emotions.

247. The broadening of the scope of a job by expanding the number of different tasks to be performed is called?
a. Job infusion.
b. Job enlargement.
c. Job enrichment.

d. Job extinction.

248. A training group scored 60 on a pre-test, and 80 on a post-test. By how much has the training increased participants' knowledge?
a. 0.03%
b. 60%
c. 160%
d. 33.3%

249. Which of the following is not required by IRCA?
a. I-9 forms be completed for all new employees within 3 days of hire.
b. Employers comply with IRCA in good faith.
c. I-9 forms be maintained for all employees.
d. I-9 forms be maintained for 5 years.

250. The best reason to keep a log of an employee's performance is to:
a. Provide support and/or backup and reduce rater errors.
b. Make employees aware that their performance is documented.
c. Make employees aware of areas where improvement is needed.
d. Satisfy requirements of federal laws.

251. Programs developed to assist displaced employees in finding jobs and adjusting to change are called?
a. Outplacement programs.
b. Weingarten programs.
c. WARN derivatives.
d. None of the above.

252. In a strategy of job enlargement, the employee:
a. Performs additional operations of a similar type.
b. Moves from one role to another, increasing the employee's skills.
c. Is given continuous feedback and the opportunity to improve performance.
d. Shifts between tasks requiring a short and long work cycle to improve task flexibility.

253. Re-integrating employees into their home-country operations following an international assignment is called?
a. Integration programs.
b. Repatriation.
c. Expatriation.
d. All of the above.

254. Which of the following is not a Union ULP?
a. Mass picketing in such numbers that non-striking employees are physically barred from entering the plant.
b. Threats to employees that they will lose their jobs unless they support the union's activities.
c. An employer threatens to take away an employee's job or benefits if that person should join or vote for a union.

d. Fining employees for crossing a picket line after they resigned from the union.

255. A type of bargaining based on four premises: 1) separate the people from the problem, 2) focus on interests, not positions, 3) invent options for mutual gain, and 4) insist on objective criteria; is called?
a. Parallel bargaining.
b. Distributive bargaining.
c. Pattern bargaining.
d. Principled bargaining.

256. When the NLRB does not allow an election because a bargaining unit is covered by a valid collective-bargaining agreement, this is what type of election bar?
a. Prior Petition Bar.
b. Blocking charge bar.
c. Contract Bar.
d. Statutory Bar.

257. Which of the following Acts limited the use of injunctions to break strikes and exempted unions from the Sherman Antitrust Act of 1890?
a. Clayton Act.
b. Wagner Act.
c. Labor Management Relations Act.
d. Landrum-Griffith Act.

258. The Dodd-Frank Wall Street Reform and Consumer Protection Act 2010 places major regulations on the financial industry. Which of these was not established by the Act?
a. The Consumer Financial Protection Bureau.
b. Public Company Accounting Oversight Board.
c. The Financial Stability Oversight Council.
d. Whistleblowers may receive from 10 to 30% of the proceeds from a litigation settlement.

259. The Labor Management Relations Act (LMRA) grants the President the right to obtain an injunction to end a strike for a _____ day cooling-off period?
a. 90.
b. 80.
c. 70.
d. 60.

260. Which of the following is NOT one of Porter's 5 forces?
a. Threat of new entrants.
b. Threat of changing cultures.
c. Substitute products or services.
d. Bargaining power of buyers.

261. A major deficiency of most performance appraisal systems in developing employees is the lack of:
a. Supervisory training in how to assign performance ratings.

b. Consistent and fair rating of all employees.
c. Action planning and follow-up based on performance ratings.
d. Behavior-based rating factors in the appraisal system.

262. Which of the following is NOT an environmental scanning tool?
a. SWOT Analysis.
b. PEST Analysis.
c. Employee survey.
d. Porter's 5 forces.

263. An organization structure where there are multiple reporting lines is called?
a. Matrix structure.
b. Geographic structure.
c. Divisional structure.
d. Seamless organization.

264. Which of the following Acts prohibit American companies from making corrupt payments to foreign officials for the purpose of obtaining or keeping business;
a. Fair Credit Reporting Act.
b. Foreign Corrupt Practices Act.
c. Equal Employment Opportunity Act.
d. None of the above.

265. Tobi recently received a letter stating that a prospective employer will obtain a consumer report for employment purposes, she was also asked to give written authorization for the report to be obtained. Which of the following laws requires the employer to do this?
a. Title IX.
b. Fair Credit Reporting Act.
c. Consumer Credit Protection Act (CCPA).
d. USERRA.

266. A written request asking vendors to propose solutions and prices that fit a customer's requirements is called?
a. Independent contracts.
b. Request For Proposal.
c. Consumer report.
d. Request for bidding.

267. If 2,000 homes in a residential suburb of 40,000 homes have the Lean treadmill, the market penetration of the Lean treadmill is?
a. 10%.
b. 15%.
c. 5.5%.
d. 5%.

268. What practice is most commonly followed in dealing with red-circle situations?
a. Assign the employee to a higher level job.

b. Cut the employee rate of pay to the maximum for that range.
c. Freeze the employee rate until the salary structure is sufficiently revised.
d. Increase the responsibilities of the red-circled employees in order to justify the higher salary level.

269. The Act that limits the amount of wages that can be garnished or withheld in any one week by an employer to satisfy creditors?
a. Fair Credit Reporting Act.
b. Consumer Credit Protection Act.
c. Sarbanes Oxley Act.
d. Foreign Corrupt Practices Act.

270. An organization with fewer than 25 employees who each perform unique functions would most likely develop a job evaluation system using which method?
a. Classification.
b. Factor comparison.
c. Rating.
d. Ranking.

271. An employee is covered under an organization's medical expense benefit plan (Plan A) with a $200 deductible and an 80% co-insurance provision. After being hospitalized, the total allowable medical expenses were $50,200. The employee is also covered by the spouse's plan (Plan B) as a dependent with a $100 deductible and a 70% co-insurance provision. Plans A and B have coordination of benefit (COB) provisions. What amount will the employee receive under Plan A?
a. $10,100.
b. $40,000.
c. $40,160.
d. $50,200.

272. Which of the following was set up by ERISA to insure payment of benefits in the event that a private-sector defined benefit pension plan terminates with insufficient funds to pay the benefits?
a. Department of Labor.
b. Workforce Pension Plan.
c. Pension Benefit Guaranty Corporation.
d. Employee Pension Committee.

273. Greater flexibility for employees can be built into a vacation leave program by:
a. Providing more vacation time.
b. Reducing the advance notice period.
c. Assigning leave time based on seniority.
d. Having supervisors assign leave dates.

274. Which of the following eliminates the duplication of payments when an employee, spouse, or dependents have health coverage under two or more plans?
a. Coordination of benefits.
b. Fee for service.

c. Time-based coordination.
d. IRA Intervention.

275. What is the principal advantage of an employer maintaining a qualified pension plan as opposed to a nonqualified plan?
a. Approved by the Social Service Administration.
b. Better Pension Benefit Guaranty Corporation (PBGC) insurance rates.
c. Decreased administrative costs.
d. Tax advantages for the employee and employer.

276. A system by which qualified retirement plan participants become incrementally vested over a period of years of service is called?
a. Cliff vesting.
b. Graded vesting.
c. 401(k) vesting.
d. 403 b vesting.

277. Which of the following is not one of the four leadership styles described in the Path-Goal Theory by Robert House?
a. Productive.
b. Directive.
c. Supportive.
d. Participative.

278. Which of the following leadership theories provides four styles of leadership which are telling, selling, participating and delegating?
a. Least Preferred Coworker theory.
b. Blake-Mouton Managerial Grid.
c. Path-Goal Theory.
d. Hersey-Blanchard Theory.

279. A female employee was hired to serve as an Assistant Manager in a retail store at a salary of $600 weekly. Her male counterpart, who performs the same work requiring equal skill and effort under similar working conditions, earns $500 per week. If the employer above decides to correct the situation by paying the male $50 per week more than his female counterpart, under the Equal Pay Act, the employer:
a. may be required to recruit at the higher pay to show good faith.
b. can pay a differential to retain the male employee.
c. implement a broadbanding system to prevent future occurrences.
d. may have to defend against a prima facie case of discrimination.

280. Which organization enforces the Sarbanes-Oxley Act provision of protection for employees who report illegal activities of their employers (whistle-blowers)?
a. Securities and Exchange Commission.
b. Occupational Safety and Health Administration.
c. Wage and Hour Division.
d. Department of Labor.

281. An employee can change a Section 125 deduction during the plan year in which of the following circumstances?
a. The employee experiences financial hardship.
b. A qualifying change in family status occurs within 30 days.
c. The money is to be used for continued education.
d. The employee's implements an after-tax deduction.

282. Which of the following will be a motivating factor for an employee at the safety needs level of Abraham Maslow's Hierarchy of Needs?
a. Accolades from peers.
b. Teamwork.
c. Job security.
d. Supervisory training.

283. Jobs used as reference points when setting up a job classification system and when designing or modifying a pay structure are called?
a. Classification jobs.
b. Benchmark jobs.
c. Modified jobs.
d. Structured jobs.

284. Which of the following is an example of a nonqualified deferred compensation plan?
a. Cash balance plan.
b. Excess deferral plan.
c. Money purchase plan.
d. Target benefit plan.

285. Which of the following is an arrangement in which an employee is paid a portion of their income at a later stage in life?
a. Conferred pay.
b. Deferred pay.
c. Incentives.
d. Restricted options.

286. Which of the following acts requires that companies with federal construction contracts pay their laborers the minimum wage of employees in the geographic area in which the work is being performed?
a. McNamara-O'Hara Service Act.
b. Davis-Bacon Act.
c. Walsh-Healey Act.
d. Fair Labor Standard Act.

287. What Act requires all government contractors with contracts exceeding $10,000 to pay their employees the real, prevailing wage for their locality, as established by the Secretary of Labor?
a. Service Contract Act.
b. McNamara-O'Hara Act.
c. Fair Labor Standards Act.

d. Walsh-Healey Public Contracts Act.

288. Employers are required to grant which of the following employees FMLA leave with the understanding that the employee will be reinstated after the leave?
a. An employee of a company with 400 employees who wants to stay home during the summer with a newly adopted son, age 5.
b. A CFO of a Fortune 500 company whose spouse is terminally ill.
c. A secretary who works for a firm with 25 employees and is expecting a baby.
d. A nonexempt employee of a large corporation who wants to take a vacation with a parent.

289. Which of the following is required annually by the Employee Retirement Income Security Act to ensure that highly compensated employees do not receive greater benefits from a company's 401k plan than the benefits received by other employees?
a. Administrative services test.
b. Actual deferral percentage test.
c. Vesting test.
d. Fiduciary survey.

290. Which of these laws was NOT created specifically to address occupational safety and health issues?
a. OSHA
b. MSHA
c. Drug-Free Workplace Act.
d. WARN Act.

291. Under COBRA, participants may be required to pay 100% of monthly premiums as well as an administration fee not to exceed:
a. 2%
b. 3%
c. 4%
d. 6%

292. Which of the following is not one of the five phases of a project life cycle?
a. Information.
b. Planning.
c. Executing.
d. Controlling.

293. Which of the following is NOT a benefit to diversity in the workplace?
a. Increased candidate pool.
b. Improved creativity.
c. Reflects the population.
d. Reduces worker's compensation claims.

294. Which of these is NOT one of the six core principles of the SHRM Code of Ethical and professional Standards in Human Resource Management?
a. Professional responsibility.

b. Ethical Leadership.
c. Inclusion & Diversity.
d. Use of Information.

295. The following are examples of quantitative analysis tools except?
a. Simulation models.
b. Ratios.
c. Delphi technique.
d. Time-series forecasts.

296. Which of these is not a central tendency measure?
a. Mean.
b. Ratio.
c. Weighted average.
d. Moving average.

297. An advantage of flexible compensation programs is that they:
a. Have low operating costs.
b. Recognize employee needs.
c. Carry low risk of discrimination.
d. Are easily administered.

298. Which of the following is not an example of a tactical accountability metric?
a. Training cost per employee.
b. Return On Investment.
c. Grievance rates.
d. Cost per hire.

299. The IRS 20-Factor Test is used to determine?
a. If an employee is a highly compensated employee.
b. If an individual is an employee or an independent contractor.
c. If an employee has been taxed according to FICA.
d. If an employee is to pay unemployment insurance.

300. An EEO-1 report must be filed if ___ employees are working for a private employer?
a. 20.
b. 40.
c. 100.
d. 50.

Section 3 Answers and Explanations

201. B. *A positive correlation means there is a relationship between two things and they move in the same direction. A positive correlation between the software test scores and job performance means that the top performing employees scored higher on the test. A negative correlation is a relationship between two variables such that as the value of one variable increases, the other decreases, e.g if the better-performing employees scored lower on the test, that will be a negative correlation.*

202. C. *Golden handcuffs refer to benefits which are deferred payments, provided by an employer to discourage an employee from taking employment elsewhere.*

203. B. Corporate social responsibility (CSR) refers to business practices that involve participating in initiatives that benefit society.

204. C. Individuals working under F-1 student visas are only allowed to work in the U.S. on a temporary basis. They are still required to pay federal and state income taxes but are not required to have Social Security/Medicare taxes since they will not be in the USA on a long-term basis and will not use those benefits at retirement.

205. B. Edwards Deming introduced the management theory Total Quality Management (TQM). TQM states that quality is defined by the customer and production is to be aligned to meet customer needs.

206. A. The definition above is best suited to an assessment center which assesses a candidate's suitability for a job through various tasks and activities that allow an employer to test skills that aren't necessarily accessible in a traditional interview.

207. C. The employer's initial concern is the requirements of the Worker Adjustment and Retraining Notification Act (WARN) which requires employers to provide 60 days advance notice of certain plant closings and mass layoffs. The ADEA allows employers to observe the terms of a bona fide seniority system, i.e. "last in, first out" which usually favors older employees.

208. D. The Labor Management Reporting and Disclosure Act (LMRDA) placed controls on internal union operations and gave employees the right to sue the union. The Norris-La Guardia Act outlawed yellow dog contracts. The NLRA or Wagner Act is referred to as the labor bill of rights while the Railway Labor Act covers railroad and airline companies.

209. A. The question above refers to a psychomotor assessment test. Cognitive ability tests assess reasoning and problem solving abilities.

210. A. Exit interviews are tools organizations use to gather valuable information about the reasons employees leave. When exit interview data is reviewed, this will determine if pay, benefits or other factors contribute towards employee turnover.

211. B. A weighted employment application form gives aspects of the job that are more important for success a higher weight than other areas, usually by assigning numerical values to different areas.

212. C. The Unemployment Compensation Amendments of 1992; NOT OBRA; requires that 20% income tax be withheld from some distributions to rollover accounts.

213. A. Executive Order 11246 prohibits federal contractors who do over $10,000 in Government business in one year from committing employment-related discrimination. It also requires government contractors to have a written affirmative action plan who have contracts of $50,000 or more and 50 employees or more.

214. B. The Small Business Job Protection Act of 1996 helped to simplify ADP tests for 401(k) plans and redefined highly compensated employees for small enterprises.

215. B. A vacancy should not express a preference for candidates listed as protected classes such as race, sex, age, color etc. Acceptable information should be job related in all circumstances.

216. C. The Retirement Equity Act (REA) lowered age limits for participation and vesting in pension plans. REA also requires qualified pension plans to provide automatic survivor benefits and allow for waiver of survivor benefits only with the consent of the participant and the spouse.

217. C. Job candidates are protected from employment discrimination based on disability under the Americans with Disabilities Act (ADA). The employer who refuses to interview the applicant can be sued for

discrimination. A mental disability may not mean the individual will harm someone else, which is what negligent hiring refers to.

218. C. COBRA allows for an employee who is disabled within 60 days of a reduction in hours to be eligible for the general 18 months plus an additional 11 months of COBRA coverage totaling 29 months.

219. A. Behavioral interview questions are designed to learn more about how an individual might act in the future based on how they have handled incidents in the past. Situational interview questions are similar to behavioral questions, but instead of asking you to relay a past experience and tell how you handled yourself in that situation, you're presented with a hypothetical situation.

220. D. A needs assessment is not legally required for a sexual harassment training. Federal law does not require supervisor or employee sexual harassment prevention training, although such training helps reduce incidences of sexual harassment in the workplace.

221. A. Vicarious liability refers to a situation where someone is held responsible for the actions of another. An employer can be liable for the acts of its employees in the course of their employment. A common example is sexual harassment in the workplace where the employer may be held liable for the actions of the harassing employee.

222. B. Any employee pay or benefits not regarded as wages and salaries falls under the term Indirect compensation. This includes legally required benefits such as Social Security, Medicare or FMLA.

223. A. Construct validity determines whether a test measures characteristics that are important for being able to perform a job. Criterion-related validity is measured by comparing the scores on a selection test to a particular aspect of job performance.

224. B. Forced distribution also known as forced ranking requires managers to rate employees according to a bell curve, rating a small group at the high end, a small group at the low end and the bulk of employees in the average level.

225. A. In-basket exercises is when an individual is given a stack of business papers and has to prioritize the items and make decisions about them. These are used at assessment centers, along with role plays, mock interviews and presentations, to evaluate individuals' suitability for management positions.

226. C. Content validity is a measure of job knowledge or skill which involves having someone perform actual work tasks or taking a test of job knowledge such as a practical driving test.

227. C. Last hired, first fired policies use a seniority system to determine who will be laid off first if layoffs become necessary.

228. A. The S-shaped learning curve is a combination of positive and negative learning curve with series of increases and decreases in learning.

229. C. Cross-training is the act of teaching employees the skills and responsibilities of other positions. It can result in employers having more staffing flexibility and teamwork amongst employees.

230. B. The results evaluation method provides the most valuable feedback to the business. It seeks to determine the impact of the training on business results and the bottomline.

231. D. Behavior modeling is the act of copying what someone else does. It is a useful way to help people learn and apply good relationship-building and communication skills. It is used most effectively for training new supervisors and managers.

232. C. The continuous feedback program is the most effective method of evaluating employee performance. By consistently addressing performance on an ongoing basis, employees are given the consistent support and feedback they need to achieve success.

233. B. There are four widely recognized phases of training evaluation: reaction, learning, behavior and results. Organizations rush into designing, developing and implementing training for employees without taking time to plan for the evaluation phase of training. If evaluation is not considered at the planning stage, it may be difficult to ascertain achievement of the desired objective.

234. A. Learning evaluation seeks to measure what the trainees have learned and how much their knowledge has increased as a result of the training.

235. D. The retail store cannot advertise for a young Asian lady as that will be discrimination based on age and race; race and color can never be BFOQs. The age requirement for bus drivers and airline pilots is backed by statutes.

236. D. The best way to measure the effectiveness of a training program is through the four stages of evaluation: reaction, learning, behavior and results. The only way to do this is to put a pilot group through the training. A focus group will only deliberate on the training not participate while a pre-session survey will only be able to capture participants' expectations of training. The delphi technique is method of group decision-making and forecasting that involves successively collating the judgments of experts but is not useful in ensuring training effectiveness.

237. B. Kinesthetic learners are hands-on, experiential learners who learn best by doing.

238. B. One way to learn how to make sales is to observe someone else going through the process of working with a customer to close a deal. Studying the sales manual and/or attending seminars on interdepartmental interactions and credit may be useful but they are not training strategies which are most likely to improve results.

239. C. The knowledge of predictor bias is based on prior knowledge or an awareness of performance indicators such as an assessment test.

240. D. Team-building efforts are not likely to be perceived by employees as unnecessary when management is involved and actively encourages such activities

241. D. The FLSA requires that non-discretionary bonuses must be included in the regular rate of pay to compute overtime pay. For referral bonuses, conditions in option A, B and C must be met.

242. B. The behaviorally anchored rating scale (BARS) approach to performance appraisal requires an in-depth understanding of each position's key tasks, along with an understanding of the full range of behaviors displayed by individuals in carrying out such task. Therefore, the scales are tailored to the required behaviors rather than to the nature of work.

243. A. Blended learning combines classroom learning with online learning, in which students can, in part, control the time, pace, and place of their learning. Computer-based training (CBT) is any course of instruction whose primary means of delivery is a computer. A Socratic seminar is a formal discussion in which the leader asks open-ended questions while students listen and think critically for themselves.

244. B. Remember that for purposes of calculating overtime pay, the FLSA provides that non-discretionary bonuses must be included in the regular rate of pay. Non-discretionary bonuses include those that are announced to employees to encourage them to work more steadily, rapidly or efficiently, and bonuses designed to encourage employees to remain with a facility.
Step 1: $200 (Bi-weekly attendance bonus) / 2 = $100 (Weekly Bonus Equivalent) ;
Step 2: 60 hours worked * $13/hour + $100 (Weekly Bonus Equivalent) = $880 (Total Standard Compensation) ;
Step 3: $880 (Total Standard Compensation) / 60 hours worked = $14.67 (regular rate) ;
Step 4: $14.67 (regular rate) * ½ = $7.34 (half-time premium) ;
Step 5: $14.67 (regular rate) + $7.34 (half-time premium) = $22.01 (overtime rate);
Step 6: 40 (straight time hours) * $14.67 (regular rate) = $586.80 (straight time earnings) ;
Step 7: 20 (overtime hours) * $22.01 (overtime rate) = $440.20 (overtime earnings);

Step 8: Oke's total earning for Week 9 = $586.80 + $440.20 = $1,027.
Remember the productivity bonus is bi-weekly, so the figure is divided by 2 to get the weekly bonus equivalent.

245. C. The most important outcome for a new employee is effective work performance. Therefore, supervisory feedback is essential at that stage.

246. A. Emotional Intelligence is the ability to identify and manage your own emotions and the emotions of others.

247. B. Job enlargement means increasing the scope of a job through extending the range of its job duties and responsibilities generally within the same level. It is different from Job enrichment which involves redesigning jobs so that they are more challenging to the employee and have less repetitive work.

248. D. Subtract the pre-test score from the post-test score and then divide it by the pre-test score to get the percentage difference: 80 - 60 = 20; 20 divided by 60 = .33 or 33.3%.

249. D. The Immigration Reform and Control ACt, the IRCA requires that the employee section of the I-9 form be completed by the end of the first day of employment while the employer section be completed by the end of the 3rd day of employment. The IRCA requires that I-9 forms be maintained for 3 years from date of hire or 1 year from the date of termination not for 5 years.

250. A. An employee performance log helps supervisors document the good and bad aspects of an employee's performance. It is a useful reminder for managers to provide feedback and helps ensure consistency and recordkeeping.

251. A. Outplacement programs are the efforts made by a downsizing company to help former employees transition to new jobs and help them re-orient themselves to the job market.

252. A. Job enlargement means giving employees more same-level duties and tasks without a change of pay or title; it is a horizontal expansion. Job enrichment means giving an employee additional responsibilities previously reserved for his manager or other higher-ranking positions.

253. B. Repatriation is the process of returning an employee to his or her place of origin or citizenship after an international assignment.

254. C. Option C is an Employer Unfair Labor Practice (ULP) not a Union ULP.

255. D. Principled bargaining is the interest-based approach to negotiation as described by Roger Fisher and William Ury; they advocate for four fundamental principles of negotiation as stated above.

256. C. The contract bar doctrine provides that once a contract is executed, the National Labor Relations Board (NLRB) generally does not permit a representation election in the unit covered by the contract until the contract expires up to a 3 year limit.

257. A. The Clayton Act limited the use of injunctions to break strikes and exempted unions from the Sherman Antitrust Act.

258. B. The Dodd-Frank Act of 2010 was passed as a response to the financial crisis of 2008. It established the Consumer Financial Protection Bureau (CFPB) to examine and enforce regulations for banks and credit unions with assets of over $10 billion and all mortgage-related businesses; it established the Financial Stability Oversight Council to identify and takes steps to address systemic risks to the nation's financial system; it strengthened the whistleblower program by establishing a mandatory bounty program under which whistleblowers can receive from 10 to 30% of the proceeds from a litigation settlement. The Public Company Accounting Oversight Board was established by the Sarbanes-Oxley Act (SOX) of 2002.

259. B. The LMRA or the Taft-Hartley Act allows for an 80-day suspension of a strike which, after investigation, the President of the U. S. has found to be creating a national emergency. The injunction does not last for more than 80 days, during which it is expected that the parties will negotiate a settlement of the strike. The strike may legally resume after this 80-day "cooling-off period."

260. B. Porter's 5 forces analysis is a framework that is used for business strategy development by analysing 5 competitive forces within an industry. The 5 forces are threat of new entrants, threat of substitute products and services, bargaining power of buyers, bargaining power of suppliers and threat of established rivals.

261. C. Performance appraisals are used primarily as a means of documenting employee performance and allocating bonuses. Although many performance appraisal methods include developmental goals for the following year, these goals are only for record-keeping rather than as a tool to guide future planning and feedback discussions.

262. C. Environmental scanning is a process that systematically surveys and interprets relevant data to identify external opportunities and threats. Option C is not an environmental scanning tool.

263. A. Explanation: In a matrix structure, employees report to two or more managers. Traditional hierarchies do not exist in a seamless organization. A geographic structure exists where there are executives of regional areas for all business functions. The divisional structure is a type of organizational structure that groups each organizational function into a division.

264. B. The Foreign Corrupt Practices Act of 1977 was enacted for the purpose of making it unlawful for certain classes of persons and entities to make payments to foreign government officials to assist in obtaining or retaining business.

265. B. The Fair Credit Reporting Act is a Federal government legislation enacted to promote the accuracy, fairness, and privacy of consumer information contained in the files of consumer reporting agencies. Employers are required to disclose and receive written authorization from a candidate before obtaining consumer reports for employment purposes. The CCPA's title III details restrictions on wage garnishment.

266. B. A Request for proposal (RFP) is a solicitation made through a bidding process by a company interested in procurement of a commodity, service or valuable asset, to potential suppliers to submit business proposals.

267. D. The Market penetration formula is the number of people who buy or use a product divided by the relevant market size *100 to be expressed as a percentage.

268. C. An employee is considered to be "red-circled" when their rate of pay is higher than the maximum rate of pay allowed by their pay grade.

269. B. The Consumer Credit Protection Act (CCPA) details wage garnishment provisions to protect employees from discharge by their employers because their wages have been garnished for any one debt, and it limits the amount of an employee's earnings that may be garnished in any one week.

270. D. Job evaluation is the process of measuring the worth of a job compared to other jobs. This helps organizations pay people appropriately based on the overall value of their jobs to the organization. Ranking is the best option for a small organization because it is easy; jobs are simply placed in order based on their value to the organization.

271. B. A deductible is an amount designated by a particular insurance plan which an employee or dependent must pay before the insurance will cover expenses. Co-insurance is the portion of covered expenses that insurance will pay after a deductible is met. The remaining percentage is the responsibility of the employee. Therefore, in this example, the employee is responsible for $200 (deductible) of the $50,200 charge. Their insurance (Plan A) will then pay 80% of the remaining $50,000, which is $40,000.

272.   C. The Pension Benefit Guaranty Corporation (PBGC) provides a safety net for participants in private-sector defined-benefit plans (not for defined contribution plans) by insuring the participants' benefits under the plan. The PBGC was established by the Employee Retirement Income Security Act (ERISA) of 1974 to give participants in plans covered by the PBGC guaranteed "basic" benefits in the event that their employer-sponsored defined benefit plans become insolvent.

273.   B. Vacation leave programs are voluntary time off programs offered by employers. Employees are usually expected to request time off from their supervisors. If employees must request time off months in advance this may inhibit an employee's ability to take time off for spontaneous family visits or other activities. Reducing the advance notice period will give employees greater flexibility.

274.   A. Coordination of benefits helps ensure that members covered by more than one plan will receive the benefits they are entitled to while avoiding overpayment by either plan.

275.   D. A qualified retirement plan is one that gives employers a tax break for the contributions they make for employees if the plan satisfies a set of specific requirements. Similarly, employees who contribute to such a plan can reduce their current tax liability by reducing their taxable income.

276.   B. Graded vesting is the process by which employees gain a certain percentage of irrevocable rights over employer contributions made to the employee's retirement plan account each year until the employee is fully vested.

277.   A. The Path-Goal Theory states that a leader is to establish goals and provide directions on reaching the goals. Robert House described 4 leadership styles used to accomplish goals; Directive, Supportive, Participative and Achievement-oriented. Productive leadership is not one of them.

278.   D. Hersey-Blanchard theory describes leadership in terms of the maturity level of the followers. It provides four leadership styles which are telling, selling, participating and delegating.

279.   D. According to the Equal Employment Opportunity Commission (EEOC), a prima facie (Latin for "first impression") violation of the Equal Pay Act (EPA), occurs when it can be shown that a male and female employee receive unequal compensation for substantially equal jobs within the same establishment. The employer in this case believes that paying the male employee more than the female employee will make up for the low pay the male employee had been receiving. However, in doing so they will be paying the male employee more than the female employee, which is a prima facie violation. Broadbanding is a pay grade method designed primarily to flatten an organizational structure and will not solve the problem.

280.   B. Whistleblowers are protected by the Sarbanes-Oxley Act from retaliation, enforcement of this protection is handled by OSHA.

281.   B. A Section 125 plan, also known as a flexible spending plan, allows participants to set aside funds to pay for qualifying medical expenses. The structure of the plan allows employees to reduce their taxable income in the process. This means that such plans have to follow IRS rules, one of which is that an employee cannot change their mind once they decide how much money they want to set aside for a plan year. The exception is if there are certain "changes in status" which occur such as marriage, divorce, birth or death. Financial hardship and the other factors listed have no bearing on such plans.

282.   C. Maslow's hierarchy of needs states that people aim to meet basic needs and then seek to meet successively higher needs in the form of a pyramid. These needs are physiological, safety, social, esteem and self-actualization needs. An employee at the safety needs level will be motivated by job security.

283.   B. Benchmark jobs are those with a clear and consistent definition in the relevant labor market, for which reliable market data can be collected.

284.   B. Non-qualified deferred compensation plans are not protected by ERISA and provide retirement funds that supplement qualified retirement benefits. Three types of nonqualified plans are grantor/rabbi trusts, top-hat plans and excess deferral plans.

285. B. Deferred pay or deferred compensation is an arrangement in which a portion of an employee's income is paid out at a later date after which the income was actually earned. Examples of deferred compensation include pensions, retirement plans, and employee stock options.

286. B. The Davis Bacon Act requires that companies with federal <u>construction</u> contracts must pay the minimum wages to workers who provide construction work on federal or public work projects that are in excess of $2,000.

287. D. Walsh-Healey Public Contracts Act of 1936 requires government contractors with contracts exceeding $10,000 (for other than construction work) to pay their employees the prevailing wage for their local area.

288. A. FMLA (the Family and Medical Leave Act) requires employers with 50 or more employees to grant eligible employees up to 12 weeks of unpaid leave for medical leave and similar reasons. The CFO can be denied reinstatement from leave as a "key employee," The secretary works for a small (less than 50 employees)company which is not required to provide FMLA leave and the nonexempt employee wants to take a vacation rather than to care for a parent with a serious health condition. Therefore, the only employee eligible among those listed is the employee who just adopted a child since adoption is a protected form of leave.

289. B. ERISA requires an Actual Deferral Percentage (ADP) test each year to check that employees who are considered to be highly compensated do not receive greater 401(k) benefits than other employees.

290. D. The WARN Act, the Worker Adjustment and Retraining Notification Act addresses plant closing and mass layoffs, it does not address workplace safety issues.

291. A. COBRA (the Consolidated Omnibus Budget Reconciliation Act) requires certain employers with group health plans to give employees and/or their dependents the right to stay on the organization's health plan even if something occurs that would make them ineligible for the plan, such as termination of employment or divorce. Employees pay the full premium cost and can also be charged an administrative fee of up to 2% of the premium.

292. A. The five phases of a project life cycle are initiation, planning, executing, controlling and closing.

293. D. Workers' compensation laws protect people who are injured on the job. They are designed to ensure that employees who are injured or disabled on the job are provided with fixed monetary awards, eliminating the need for litigation, diversity has no impact on workers' compensation claims.

294. C. The six core principles of the SHRM Code of Ethical and Professional Standards in HRM are Professional Responsibility, Professional Development, Ethical Leadership, Fairness and Justice, Conflicts of Interest and Use of Information. Option C is not one of the six core principles.

295. C. Quantitative analysis tools are based on mathematical models for measuring historical data. The Delphi technique is a qualitative analysis tool for gathering data from experts. The technique is designed as a group communication process which aims to achieve a convergence of opinion on a specific issue.

296. B. A ratio is a statement of how two numbers compare. It is a comparison of the size of one number to the size of another number. It is not a central tendency (or average) measure.

297. B. Flexible benefit programs, such as cafeteria plans, allow employees to choose from a "menu" of different benefit options in order to obtain the benefits they value the most. It also allows employees to choose different combinations of stable base pay and more risky variable pay. The purpose of such plans is to meet individual employee needs.

298. B. Tactical accountability metrics measure HR effectiveness and how well programs for workforce management issues, productivity and other HR activities are working. Return on Investment is a business impact measure which measures how HR programs add value to the bottom-line.

299. B. *The IRS 20-Factor Test on employment status is used to determine option B.*

300. C. *The EEO-1 report is a compliance survey mandated by federal statute. The survey requires company employment data to be categorized by race/ethnicity, gender and job category. Employers who must complete the EEO-1 report are private employers subject to Title VII with 100 or more employees and Federal contractors with 50 or more employees who have contracts or subcontracts of $50,000 or more.*

Section 4 Questions

301. Which of the following is not a major factor in establishing compensation within an organization?
a. IRS rules.
b. Employee salary history.
c. Current labor market analysis.
d. Competition salary survey.

302. What is the purpose of a total rewards strategy?
a. To represent the employee brand.
b. To use the budget for rewards in order to retain employees.
c. To establish a seniority salary philosophy.
d. To establish salary structures among employees.

303. All of the following are part of the Fair Labor Standards Act except?
a. Minimum wage.
b. Exemption condition for employees.
c. Federal Service contracts.
d. Working conditions for children.

304. Hannah has been instructed to design a training method that will allow the staff members to discuss problems and potential resolutions under the supervision of a third party expert. Which of the following instructional methods will be most effective for this training?
a. Vestibule.
b. Demonstration.
c. Facilitation.
d. Conference.

305. Which of the following is a permissible activity that unions can engage in?
a. Yellow dog contracts.
b. Salting.
c. Engaging in a ULP.
d. Jurisdictional strikes.

306. A union insists on a hot cargo clause to the employer during the collective bargaining session. This is an example of?
a. Distributive bargaining.
b. Principled bargaining.

c. Illegal bargaining.
d. Parallel bargaining.

307. The following are torts except?
a. Constructive discharge.
b. Wrongful termination.
c. Negligent hiring.
d. Employment contract.

308. A strike conducted in support of other striking unions is called?
a. Economic strike.
b. Wildcat strike.
c. Sympathy strike.
d. Common-situs strike.

309. Which of the following is NOT considered a human process intervention?
a. Redesigning jobs.
b. Team-building activities.
c. Conflict Resolution.
d. Emotional Intelligence.

310. Which of the following is NOT a statutory benefit?
a. Social security.
b. COBRA.
c. FMLA leave.
d. Stock options.

311. Adverse impact occurs when the rate of selection for a protected class is less than ___ percent of the rate for the class with the highest selection rate?
a. 70%
b. 80%
c. 20%
d. 50%

312. Under FMLA, if the leave can be reasonably anticipated, how many days notice must the employee give the employer?
a. 15 days.
b. 30 days.
c. 7 days.
d. 90 days.

313. Which of the following terms refers to collapsing multiple pay grades to produce a wide range?
a. Broadbanding.
b. Golden handcuffs.
c. Golden parachute.
d. Green circle rate.

314. If funds in a flexible spending account are not used, what happens to the funds?

a. The organization returns the funds to the employee.
b. The employee forfeits any unspent funds.
c. The funds rollover to the next year.
d. The IRS pays the funds to the employee.

315. Which of the following is used to determine current market trends in setting pay levels?
a. Compa-ratios.
b. Employee surveys.
c. Salary surveys.
d. Point-factor system.

316. The process to measure the effectiveness and efficiency of HR programs and positions is called?
a. HR audit.
b. HR Tort.
c. HR analysis.
d. HR reports.

317. The office responsible for implementing Executive Orders 11246 and ensuring Affirmative Action compliance of federal contractors?
a. EEOC.
b. OFCCP.
c. DOL.
d. NLRB.

318. The practice in which employers identify key imbalances in their workforce and take positive steps to correct underrepresentation of protected classes is called?
a. Adverse impact.
b. Affirmative action.
c. Delphi technique.
d. Concurrent validity.

319. The following are types of Bottom-Up Communication except?
a. Open-door policy.
b. Intranet.
c. Staff meetings.
d. All-hands meeting.

320. A type of horizontal organization connected by networks where traditional hierarchies don't exist is called?
a. Matrix organization.
b. Divisional organization.
c. Seamless organization.
d. Operational organization.

321. In which of these stages of strategy planning does a SWOT analysis take place?
a. Environmental Scanning.
b. Strategy Formulation.

c. Strategy dissemination.
d. Strategy implementation.

322. To facilitate employee buy-in to a new compensation and benefits program, the most significant information to communicate is:
a. The new plan's procedures.
b. The consequences of not changing.
c. How the changes affect employees.
d. Specific changes from the old plan.

323. Which of the following qualifies as indirect compensation?
a. Job enrichment.
b. State-of-the-art equipment.
c. Comfortable work environment.
d. Health insurance.

324. In addressing a performance problem with an employee, it is desirable, but not essential, to:
a. clearly define the next steps in the disciplinary process.
b. specify the behaviors resulting in poor performance.
c. obtain the employee's signature on the file documents.
d. specify future performance expectations.

325. An employee tells an external EAP counselor about ongoing sexual harassment being conducted by a plant manager. The employee wants the harassment to be kept confidential. What should the EAP counselor do first?
a. Contact the EEOC and lodge a complaint against the plant manager.
b. Personally contact the plant manager to hear the other side of the story.
c. Report the alleged harassment to the HR department without using the employee's name
d. Try to convince the employee to report the sexual harassment to the HR department.

326. Which of the following job design practices broadens the scope of a job by expanding the number of different tasks to be performed?
a. Job enrichment.
b. Task identity.
c. Skill rotation.
d. Job enlargement.

327. An employer's mission statement includes:
a. Short-term needs to meet the strategic plan.
b. A statement of purpose for what the organization values.
c. Future aspirations of the organization.
d. A statement of the company's industry and competitors.

328. Direct costs to an employer include:
a. Costs of operating a program.
b. Costs for operating departments

c. Costs for operating a unit.
d. Costs for service.

329. Which of the following is not a type of training needs analyses?
a. Task analysis.
b. Organizational analysis.
c. Operations analysis.
d. Individual analysis.

330. Common forms of behaviorally experienced training include all of the following except:
a. Diversity training.
b. In-basket techniques.
c. Apprenticeship.
d. Case studies/incidents.

331. Which of the following employees are covered by FMLA after 1 year of employment?
a. All employees in an organization that employs 40 people
b. New mothers who have worked less than 1,250 hours
c. Veterans who have worked a minimum of 1,040 hours
d. Temporary employees who have worked more than 1,250 hours

332. Which of the following is a funding feature of a health plan?
a. Self-insurance.
b. Insurance coverage.
c. HMO insurance.
d. All of the above.

333. An employee who holds a non-exempt position under the Fair Labor Standards Act:
a. Exercises discretionary authority for independent judgement.
b. Uses the percentage of his or her time performing routine, manual, or clerical work.
c. Earns $455 per week.
d. Performs outside sales functions.

334. Executives typically receive;
a. Only incentives and perquisites.
b. Sarbanes-Oxley review of pay every quarter.
c. A higher percentage of their direct compensation in base salary.
d. A wider variety of compensation programs than do other employees.

335. Direct compensation includes which of the following?
a. Section 125 plan.
b. Commissions.
c. Workers' Compensation.
d. Equity based programs.

336. Which is not one of the six levels of learning by Bloom?
a. Competence.
b. Knowledge.

c. Application.
d. Analysis.

337. Which is not one of the four criteria for evaluating training programs?
a. Reactions.
b. Apprenticeship.
c. Behavior.
d. Results.

338. What is organizational due process?
a. A mandatory bargaining topic
b. A process monitored by the NLRB
c. A requirement for all union shop organizations
d. A procedure for handling employee complaints

339. Which of the following is an example of payment that is consistent from period to period regardless of the number of hours worked?
a. Wages.
b. Bonus.
c. Salary.
d. Improshare.

340. Similarity in pay for jobs requiring comparable level of skill, responsibility and effort even where actual job duties differ significantly is called?
a. Pay equity.
b. Equal Pay.
c. Competence Pay.
d. None of the above.

341. The Pregnancy Discrimination Act of 1978 specifically regulates:
a. Employee career planning following pregnancy.
b. Hazardous occupations in which women can be employed.
c. Employment conditions and employee benefits.
d. Length of maternity and adoption leaves.

342. Which of the following is not an exemption of The Equal Pay Act?
a. Seniority.
b. Merit.
c. Production quantity.
d. Age.

343. A benefit statutorily offered by employers to employees who lose their job is called?
a. Severance Pay.
b. Outplacement benefit.
c. COBRA.
d. Employee Assistance Program (EAP).

344. An employer can use which of the following to counter a charge of sex discrimination?

a. BFOQ and business necessity defenses.
b. BFOQ and ADA defenses.
c. Business necessity and ADA defenses.
d. ADEA and adverse impact defenses.

345. Which of the following acts deals directly with discrimination in compensation?
a. Fair Labor Standard Act.
b. Equal Pay Act.
c. Comparable worth.
d. Portal-to-Portal Act.

346. Which of the following categories is not an example of an exempt classification under the FLSA?
a. Professional.
b. Executive.
c. Technical.
d. Sales.

347. Which of the following would NOT typically be grounds for bypassing the progressive discipline procedure before dismissal?
a. Chronic tardiness or absenteeism.
b. Fraudulent misrepresentation of financial statements.
c. Knowingly falsifying expense reports.
d. Fiduciary profiteering.

348. Which of the following employees must be paid overtime?
a. A construction worker who worked 35 hours during the workweek and was also paid for 12 hours of vacation time.
b. A sales senior executive who worked 50 hours last week.
c. A temporary employee who put in 42 hours last week.
d. A dock worker who worked 40 hours, including 10 hours on Thanksgiving.

349. Which of these Acts was set up to protect shareholders from accounting errors, fraudulent practices and improve corporate disclosures?
a. Securities Act of 1933.
b. Sarbanes-Oxley Act of 2002
c. Investment Advisers Act of 1940
d. Accounting Oversight Act

350. Tim has been nominated to join the Board of Directors of Grit Company because he will bring an independent perspective, strategic thinking, experience and objectivity to the Board. Tim is most likely a/an?
a. Inside director.
b. Outside director.
c. Ethical director.
d. Chief Audit Officer

351. The following are attributes of a fiduciary responsibility except?
a. Act solely in a principal's interests.

b. May not profit from their principals' without consent.
c. Analysis of conflict of interest situations.
d. Employ the strictest duty of care.

352. Which of the following is not one of the essential elements of a retirement plan under ERISA?
a. A written plan that describes the benefit structure and guides day-to-day operations.
b. A trust fund to hold the plan's assets.
c. A recordkeeping system to track the flow of monies in a rabbi trust.
d. Documents to provide plan information to employees participating in the plan.

353. The following were put in place by the Sarbanes-Oxley Act of 2002 except?
a. Established the Public Company Accounting Oversight Board (PCAOB)
b. Requires corporate investors to register with the Securities and Exchange Commission.
c. Requires all financial reports to include an Internal Controls Report.
d. Established standards of government responsibility for corporate accounting failures.

354. The following are the three main factors of the Hay system except?
a. Accountability.
b. Know-how.
c. Problem solving.
d. Competence.

355. Remi has reached the maximum contribution limit for her 401(k) workplace savings plan. Which of the following can Remi pick to save more for her retirement goals?
a. Cash balance plan.
b. Money-Purchase plan.
c. Excess deferral plan.
d. Point of Service plan.

356. Which of the following rulings has been made by the NLRB regarding pension plan development?
a. A unionized employer cannot install or terminate a pension plan covering union employees without agreement with the union.
b. An organization must obtain a union's vote on all decisions regarding pension plan administration.
c. Employers have the right to create or cancel a pension plan without the union's input.
d. All unionized employers must offer some type of pension plan.

357. An audit & review of the services and costs billed by health-care providers is known as;
a. Process review.
b. Utilization review.
c. Operational review.
d. Benefit control.

358. Under the Federal Unemployment Tax Act, the maximum FUTA tax rate is ---- percent of each worker's first -------- earned in a year.
a. 6.0 ; $7,000.

b. 0.6 ; $7,000.
c. 6.2 ; $7,000.
d. 5.4 ; $5,000.

359. Which of the following can make an individual ineligible for unemployment benefits?
a. A layoff.
b. Downsizing.
c. Being an independent contractor.
d. Constructive discharge.

360. The federal law that requires employers to withhold three separate taxes from the wages paid to employees is called?
a. Family and Medical Leave Act (FMLA).
b. Federal Unemployment Tax Act (FUTA).
c. Federal Insurance Contributions Act (FICA).
d. Social Securities Act (SSA).

361. The Summary Plan Description of an ERISA-qualified plan should include the following except?
a. When and how employees become eligible to participate.
b. Give an advance notice of FUTA rates.
c. The vesting period, i.e., the length of time an employee must belong to a plan to receive benefits from it.
d. A participant's basic rights and responsibilities under ERISA.

362. The process by which a U.S. congressional committee debates, amends, and rewrites a proposed legislation is called?
a. Holding the bill.
b. Marking up the bill.
c. Lobbying the bill.
d. Discharging the bill.

363. Which of the following HR functions is most unlikely to be outsourced?
a. Resource planning.
b. Payroll processing.
c. Workers Compensation coverage and claim.
d. Unemployment insurance.

364. Which of the following is the first step to Enterprise Risk Management?
a. What risks do we have?
b. What are the impacts of the risks?
c. How do we control the risks?
d. How do we monitor the risks?

365. Person-based pay systems means;
a. Pay systems based on job performance.
b. Pay systems based on seniority.
c. Pay systems based on the incumbent's competences and skills.
d. Pay systems based on the salary structure of the organisation.

366. Reengineering, Restructuring, Mergers and Acquisitions are all examples of?
a. Rightsizing.
b. Cost-savings.
c. Structural changes.
d. Bureaucratic processes.

367. A hybrid business structure which has both features of a partnership and corporation is called?
a. S Corporation.
b. Divestiture.
c. Limited Liability Company.
d. None of the above.

368. The OWBPA requires that:
a. Release agreements must be written in standard legal terminology.
b. Waivers can extend to rights and claims that arise after the date the waiver is executed.
c. Consideration for the waiver may include that to which the individual is already entitled.
d. Employees are advised in writing to consult with an attorney prior to signing the ADEA waiver.

369. Quid pro quo is best defined as?
a. Sexual harassment.
b. This for that.
c. Workplace Discrimination.
d. Vicarious liability.

370. The Tenni company is planning a plant closing but has refused to give its workers' 60 days advance notice of the closing as required by the WARN Act. The HR manager says the plant closing is not covered by WARN. In which of the following circumstances will the HR manager's point be valid?
a. The Tenni company has 100 or more full-time employees.
b. The Tenni company has 100 or more full and part-time employees who work a total of 4,000 hours per week.
c. The plant closing will affect 40 part-time employees.
d. The HR manager's point is not valid in any circumstance.

371. An appropriate response by employers to sexual harassment claims include;
a. Anti-harassment policies which protect from retaliation.
b. Communication and training.
c. Prompt and impartial investigation.
d. All of the above.

372. The Minks Inc. is the parent company of a food manufacturing company, a car sales company and a clothing retail outlet. The CEO of Minks Inc. wants out of the car sales company and plans to either sell it, exchange it or close it down completely. This can best be described as a?
a. Restructure.
b. Reengineering.

c. Divestiture.
d. Refinancing.

373. Which of these terms was defined by the UN Brundtland commission as "development that meets the needs of the present without compromising the ability of future generations to meet their own needs"?
a. Corporate Governance.
b. Corporate Responsibility.
c. Sustainability.
d. Stakeholder commitment.

374. A good MBO has all of the following except;
a. Goals and Objectives are bottom-up.
b. Matching Goals and Resource Allocation.
c. Established goals and objectives.
d. Periodic review of objectives.

375. The process of examining policies, procedures, documentation, systems, and practices of the HR functions with a view to identify strengths, weaknesses and issues needing resolution with the aim of improving the HR function is called?
a. HR statistics.
b. HR policy review.
c. HR risk analysis.
d. HR Audit.

376. Tayo has a disability for which he must attend physical therapy twice a month indefinitely. His employer's attendance policy allows no more than 10 absences in 12 months and Tayo is terminated after the eleventh absence. Tayo files suit, charging discrimination under the ADA. If discrimination is found by the courts, which of the following employer actions would most likely minimize liability for compensatory and punitive damages?
a. Rehire the employee and modify the work hours around the regularly scheduled therapy sessions.
b. Eliminate the position and explain to the court that it is no longer necessary.
c. Revise the attendance policy to make exceptions for ongoing therapy sessions.
d. Offer to pay for the disabled employee's past physical therapy sessions.

377. The Rehabilitation Act of 1973 prohibits discrimination on the basis of?
a. Race.
b. Disability.
c. Religion.
d. Veteran status.

378. A manager always hires young men as truck drivers. This is an example of:
a. Disparate impact.
b. Disparate treatment.
c. Sexual preference.
d. Disparate discrimination.

379. The Family Medical Leave Act requires employers having ___ employees within a ___ mile radius to provide 12 weeks of protection for qualified employees.
a. 50; 75.
b. 100; 75.
c. 75; 50.
d. 100; 5.

380. What is the maximum penalty for a willful violation under the FLSA?
a. Up to $5,000.
b. Up to $10,000.
c. Up to $70,000.
d. Up to $10,000 for overtime violations for each employee.

381. Which pre-employment process could a company use to screen candidates for employment who might pose a case of negligent hiring to the organization?
a. Reference checks.
b. Background checks.
c. Polygraph tests.
d. A and B.

382. A job can best be defined as;;
a. A group of similar positions having common tasks, duties, and responsibilities.
b. A piece-rate function.
c. A distinct, identifiable work activity composed of motions.
d. A person's work allocation at an organisation.

383. What is the maximum penalty for a willful or repeat violation under OSHA?
a. Up to $100,000.
b. Up to $70,000.
c. Up to $7,000.
d. Depends on if the hazard resulted into a fatality.

384. Variable pay is also known as;
a. Unpaid leave.
b. Performance pay.
c. Base pay.
d. Salary.

385. The NLRB receives a petition to conduct a deauthorization election. The petition has been signed by 120 of the 600 employees represented by the union in the bargaining unit. In this situation, the NLRB should:
a. Conduct the deauthorization election.
b. Have an employer-union hearing.
c. Decertify the current union representation.
d. Deny the petition.

386. A validity study, either predictive or concurrent, in which the data are statistically correlated with the criteria of performance is called?
a. Content validity.

b. Construct validity.
c. Criterion validity.
d. Concurrent validity.

387. Which of the following is an issue addressed by the Civil Rights Act of 1991?
a. International employees.
b. Race norming.
c. Consent decrees.
d. All of the above.

388. Another name for performance appraisal is?
a. Paired comparison.
b. Employee evaluation.
c. 360 degree feedback.
d. Human resources analysis.

389. An index number giving the relationship between a predictor variable and a criterion variable is called?
a. Correlation coefficient.
b. Concurrent validity.
c. Content reliability.
d. Forced ranking.

390. An organization may use a no-solicitation policy to restrict union organizing activities provided that the policy:
a. Applies to other outside non-employee organizations.
b. Has been in place for 18 months.
c. States that union ULPs will not be permitted.
d. Does not apply to non-management employees.

391. Which of the following is an example of an alternative work schedule?
a. Self-directed work teams.
b. Job rotation.
c. Job sharing.
d. Task forces.

392. The best course of action in addressing an employee's request not to work on Sundays because of religious reasons is to:
a. Explain to the employee that religious requests are not professional.
b. Deny the request because it would create an undue hardship.
c. Determine if other employees will voluntarily make schedule adjustments.
d. Approve the request due to litigation concerns.

393. Which of the following is true about job analysis?
a. Part of an affirmative action plan.
b. Produces a job description.
c. Is required by the OFCCP.
d. Is produced by a job specification.

394. In cases where ADA, FMLA, and workers' compensation laws conflict with one another, an employer should honor the:
a. Statute most beneficial to the employee.
b. Law most applicable to the situation.
c. Strictest or most severe law.
d. Statute most beneficial to the employer.

395. Which of the following is the typical method of measuring employee adherence to performance standards?
a. Quality assurance.
b. Task fulfilment.
c. Performance appraisal.
d. Productivity analysis.

396. Calculate the cost per hire of 15 employees where the internal costs adds up to 13, 000 while the external costs adds up to $47, 000?
a. $6, 000.
b. $4, 000.
c. $4, 500.
d. $5, 000.

397. Which of the following are the characteristics of change?
a. HR professionals are most often change agents.
b. Communication is key to successful change.
c. Having an executive sponsor inspires employees to commit to change.
d. All of the above.

398. Tim believes he has been discriminated against on the basis of religion; what general time limit does he have to file a charge of discrimination with the Equal Employment Opportunity Commission (EEOC)?
a. 160 days.
b. 180 days.
c. 300 days in a non-FEPA state.
d. Immediately the discrimination occurs.

399. The following are steps in forecasting except?
a. Scrutinize the current job market.
b. Anticipate employee turnover.
c. Job analysis.
d. Project future HR needs.

400. In which case did the Supreme Court hold that a charging party can prove unlawful discrimination indirectly by showing, for example, in a hiring case that: (1) the charging party is a member of a Title VII protected group; (2) he or she applied and was qualified for the position sought; (3) the job was not offered to him or her; and (4) the employer continued to seek applicants with similar qualifications.
a. Phillips v. Martin Marietta Corp.
b. Griggs v. Duke Power Co.
c. McDonnell Douglas Corp. v Green.

d. Rosenfeld v. Southern Pacific.

Section 4 Answers and Explanations

301. **B.** *When establishing compensation within an organization, considering employee salary history is not a major factor in the process.*

302. **B.** *The purpose of a total rewards strategy is one of reviewing the budget and finding out how much of the budget is available for establishing rewards that will retain employees.*

303. **C.** *The McNamara-O'Hara Service Contract Act (1965) covers federal service contracts, but the Fair Labor Standards Act does not. The FLSA covers minimum wage requirements, exemption conditions for employees, work conditions for children under 18, and overtime.*

304. **C.** *Facilitation is an instructional method that enables employees to work together on problem-solving techniques while under the guidance of a facilitator, or third-party expert in helping different groups interact effectively.*

305. **B.** *Salting is a labor union tactic involving the act of getting a job at a specific workplace with the intent of organizing a union. Salting is a legal strategy used by unions.*

306. **C.** *A clause prohibiting an employer from conducting business with some other person with whom the union has or may have a dispute. Such clauses are illegal unfair labor practices under NLRA Section 8(e). It is the Landrum-Griffith Act of 1959 (also called the Labor Management Reporting and Disclosure Act) that banned almost all hot cargo agreements (except in the garment and construction industry)*

307. **D.** *A tort is a wrongful act or an infringement of a right (other than under contract) leading to civil legal liability. An employment contract is not a tort.*

308. **C.** *A sympathy strike is one in which the strikers have no direct grievance against their own employer but attempt to support or aid another group of workers on strike. A wildcat strike is an employee work stoppage that is not authorized by the labor union to which the employees belong. An economic strike is a strike by employees over wages, hours, or working conditions..*

309. **A.** *Human process interventions are directed at developing competencies at the individual level in the organization. Job redesign is an effort where job responsibilities and tasks are reviewed, and possibly re-allocated among staff, to improve output. It is not a human process intervention.*

310. **D.** *Stock option is the right to purchase an employer's stock at a certain price, this is a voluntary benefit.*

311. **B.** *Adverse impact occurs when the selection rate for a protected class is less than 4/5ths, or 80 percent of the selection rate for the group with the highest selection rate.*

312. **B.** *When FMLA leave can be reasonably anticipated or foreseeable, the employee is to give the employer at least 30 days notice.*

313. **A.** *Broadbanding is the term applied to having extremely wide salary bands. Where a typical salary band has a 40 percent difference in pay between its minimum and maximum, broadbanding would typically have a 100 percent difference.*

314. **B.** *The IRS requires that any unused money left in an employee's FSA must be forfeited and the employer is allowed to keep the forfeited funds. Employers are now allowed to offer a grace period until March 15, or let employees carry over $500 in unused funds to the next year — although they can't do both.*

315. **C.** Salary surveys are conducted with numerous employers to determine pay levels for specific job categories and are generally conducted either by region, sector or job classification.

316. **A.** Human Resources Audit is a comprehensive method to review current HR policies, procedures and systems to identify needs for improvement of the HR function as well as to assess compliance with ever-changing rules and regulations.

317. **B.** The purpose of the Office of Federal Contract Compliance Programs (OFCCP) is to enforce the EO 11246, VEVRAA, Section 503 of the Rehabilitation Act of 1973, contractual promise of affirmative action and equal employment opportunity required of federal contractors and subcontractors.

318. **B.** Affirmative action are practices that provide equal access to employment for those groups that have been historically excluded or underrepresented, such as women and minorities.

319. **B.** A company-wide intranet constitutes an important focal point of internal communication and collaboration; however, it is a Top-Down communication method.

320. **C.** A seamless organization is one where traditional hierarchies do not exist, it is a horizontal organization connected by networks to enhance communication and creativity.

321. **A.** Environmental scanning is the framework for collecting information to create a successful strategic plan. This is the stage when the SWOT (Strength, Weakness, Opportunities, Threats) analysis takes place.

322. **C.** The most important thing to communicate to obtain employee buy-in is to provide employees with a side-by-side comparison of the old plan and the new plan to help them understand and more readily accept the changes.

323. **D.** Direct compensation refers to an employee's pay including incentive pay and overtime. Indirect compensation refers to non-monetary benefits an employee receives such as annual leave and health insurance. The other options listed are examples of intrinsic rewards -- which are non-material things that contribute to job satisfaction.

324. **C.** An employee's signature is good to have as a means of acknowledging receipt of the performance communication but not essential.

325. **D.** EAP (employee assistance program) counselors provide support and guidance to employees as needed or upon request. Confidentiality is a core element of such programs. What they can and should do is urge an employee to report the issue to their HR department so it can be investigated properly. Employer policies on sexual harassment should provide employees with confidentiality and non-retaliation as well as multiple ways to report such allegations.

326. **D.** Job enlargement means increasing the scope of a job by extending the range of its job duties and responsibilities generally within the same level and periphery. It involves combining various activities at the same level in the organization and adding them to the existing job. Job enrichment involves assigning additional responsibility normally reserved for higher level employees.

327. **B.** A vision statement expresses an organization's goal and reason for existence, while a mission statement provides an overview of the group's plans to realize that vision by identifying the service areas, target audience, values and goals of the organization.

328. **A.** Direct costs are those for activities or services that benefit specific projects, e.g., salaries for project staff and materials required for a particular project.

329. **C.** There are 3 types of training needs analyses; Organizational, task and individual. Operations analysis is not one of them.

330. C. Behaviorally experienced training provide practical training, behavior-modeling and allow the trainee to behave like he/she will in a real fashion. Apprenticeships are <u>on the job training</u> where more experienced and skilled employees train less skilled employees to acquire technical knowledge and skills.

331. D. The FMLA (Family and Medical Leave Act) states that eligible employees are those who work for a covered employer for at least 12 months at a location where the employer has at least 50 employees within 75 miles. They also must have worked at least 1,250 hours during the 12 month period immediately preceding the leave. Based on these, the first three choices are incorrect. It is immaterial whether an employee is temporary or not under the FMLA.

332. A. Health insurance are funded in two ways; Fully-Insured (there is an insurance carrier to whom the employer pays a premium vs. Self-Insured (Self-Funded, employer operates their own pension plan) Health Plans.

333. B. A nonexempt employee must be paid at least the minimum wage and overtime pay for any time worked beyond 40 hours in a given week. Such an employee will most likely engage in the functions listed in option B.

334. D. Top executives are often paid salary plus short-term performance-driven incentives and bonuses. Executive pay arrangements typically consist of six distinct compensation components: salary, annual incentives, long-term incentives, benefits, perquisites and severance/change-in-control agreement.

335. B. Direct compensation consists of four different groups of payment from the employer to the employee. They are salary, hourly pay, commissions and bonus types of wages.

336. A. Dr Benjamin Bloom's taxonomy of learning domains was created to promote higher forms of thinking in education. It identified three domains of educational activities; Cognitive, Affective and Psychomotor. There are six levels of the cognitive domain which are knowledge, comprehension, application, analysis, synthesis and evaluation.

337. B. A summative evaluation occurs at the end of a training and provides feedback of same. It has 4 criteria which are Reaction, Learning, Behavior and Results.

338. D. Under due process, employers are encouraged to build basic principles of fairness into their disciplinary procedures, such as an investigation and an opportunity for an employee to provide their side of the story.

339. C. A salary is a predetermined payment on a regular schedule which cannot be reduced because of changes in the quantity or quality of work while a wage is compensation based on the number of hours worked multiplied by an hourly rate of pay.

340. A. Pay equity, also called sex equity or <u>comparable worth is pay for work of equal value</u>; it is the principle that men and women should be compensated equally for work requiring comparable skills, responsibilities, and effort. It is different from Equal pay which requires that men and women in the same workplace be given equal pay for equal work.

341. C. The Pregnancy Discrimination Act prohibits discrimination on the basis of pregnancy, childbirth or related medical conditions as a form of unlawful sex discrimination. It does not deal with career planning, hazardous occupations or the length of leave. Instead, it states that women affected by pregnancy or related conditions must be treated in the same manner as other employees for purposes of hiring, access to leave, temporary disability and health benefits.

342. D. The Equal Pay Act allows differences in pay based on seniority systems, merit or performance, quantity or quality of production but not for differences in pay based on age.

343. C. COBRA requires continuation of health coverage to be offered to covered employees, their spouses, former spouses, and dependent children when group health coverage would otherwise be lost due to certain specific events such as job termination.

344. A. The ADA - the Americans with <u>Disabilities</u> Act has nothing to do with sex discrimination. BFOQ (bona fide occupational qualification) is a characteristic that an employer is allowed to have a preference because there is a direct business connection. For example, having a hiring preference for female clerk in a lingerie store.

345. B. The Equal Pay Act requires that men and women in the same workplace be given equal pay for equal work, thereby prohibiting compensation discrimination based on sex.

346. C. The exemption classifications under the FLSA are Executive, Administrative, Professional (Learned & Creative), Computer and Outside Sales exemptions.

347. A. Progressive discipline attempts to give employees the opportunity to correct performance or behavioral issues through a series of steps such as an oral warning, written warning etc. However, certain actions are considered unacceptable for which immediate termination is the best response such as theft and fraud.

348. C. The FLSA defines a maximum workweek for nonexempt employees as 40 hours per week. Overtime payment begins for hours that exceed 40 hours, not for work done on holidays.

349. B. The Sarbanes-Oxley Act of 2002 (SOX) protects shareholders and the general public from accounting errors, fraudulent practices in companies and improves the accuracy of corporate disclosures. The Securities Act of 1933 was set up to ensure greater transparency in financial statements for investors to make informed decisions, it also established laws against fraudulent activities in the securities markets.

350. B. Outside directors are directors who are not employees or stakeholders in a company. Outside directors bring the benefits of an unbiased opinion, contacts, independent perspective, strategic thinking and planning, experience and objectivity.

351. C. A fiduciary is an individual in whom another has placed the utmost trust and confidence to manage and protect property or money prudently. Fiduciaries are not to analyse conflict of interest situations but avoid such situations completely.

352. C. A rabbi trust is a non-qualified plan (tax-deferred, employer-sponsored retirement plan) in which funds are invested in an irrevocable trust to be held for the benefit of employees for retirement purposes. Rabbi trusts fall outside of the Employee Retirement Income Security Act (ERISA) guidelines. Non-qualified plans are designed to meet specialized retirement needs for key executives and other select employees.

353. B. The Sarbanes-Oxley Act of 2002 established the PCAOB; requires an Internal Controls Report to ensure accurate and adequate financial data and controls. It also encourages the disclosure of corporate fraud by protecting whistleblower employees but does not require corporate investors to register with the SEC.

354. D. The classification method of job evaluation has two methods; Point Factor and Hay System. The Hay system evaluates jobs based on the job content, it has three main factors, Know-how, Problem-solving and Accountability.

355. C. What Remi needs is a nonqualified deferred compensation plan, which is not subject to contribution limits or ERISA testing requirements. Only the excess deferral plan is a nonqualified deferred compensation plan.

356. A. Unionized employers must engage in collective bargaining with the union over anything that affects workers' wages, working hours and terms and conditions of employment, including benefits. Employers are not required to offer a pension plan, nor is a union entitled to vote on all aspects of plan administration. However, an employer cannot create or cancel a pension plan without union agreement.

357. B. Utilization review (UR) is a safeguard against unnecessary and inappropriate medical care. It allows healthcare providers to review patient care from perspectives of medical necessity, quality of care, appropriateness of decision-making, place of service, and length of hospital stay.

358. A. The maximum FUTA Tax Rate is 6.0% (even though in practice the FUTA tax rate is usually 0.6% when companies pay the State Unemployment Insurance in full and on time) of each worker's first $7,000 earned in a year.

359. C. To be eligible for unemployment benefits, the employer must classify the individual as an employee, and not an independent contractor because independent contractors are regarded as self-employed and not eligible for state unemployment benefits.

360. C. The Federal Insurance Contributions Act (FICA) is the federal law that requires employers to withhold three separate taxes from an employee's wages. The employer is to withhold these amounts from an employee's wages: 6.2 percent Social Security tax; 1.45 percent Medicare tax; and beginning in 2013, a 0.9 percent Medicare surtax when the employee earns over $200,000. The law also requires the employer to pay two of these taxes: a 6.2 percent Social Security tax; and the 1.45 percent Medicare tax. The employer is not required to pay the matching sum of 0.9 Medicare surtax.

361. B. The Summary Plan Description, or SPD, communicates plan rights and obligations to participants and beneficiaries. It is a summary of the material provisions of the plan document, and it should be comprehensible to to the average participant.

362. B. Markup is the process by which congressional committees and subcommittees debate, amend, and rewrite proposed bills or legislation.

363. A. Human resources planning is a process that identifies current and future human resources needs for an organization to achieve its goals. HR planning should serve as a link between human resources management and the overall strategic plan of an organization. An outside perspective may be helpful in HR planning, but only the internal team can determine current and future HR needs.

364. A. The first step in Enterprise Risk Management is to identify the risks. The question, "what risks do we have?" seeks to identify the risks.

365. C. The person-based pay or the skills-based pay compensates the job incumbent (person) in terms of his knowledge, competencies and skills rather than the job they perform. The job-based pay compensates the employee based on the compensable factors as determined by the job.

366. C. Corporate structures are formal designs of managerial hierarchies within a company which determine reporting relationships and work flows. A change in corporate structure impacts the entire business system just like the terms above will.

367. C. A Limited Liability Company (LLC) is a business structure that combines pass-through taxation, limited liability and legal protection for personal assets. It is a hybrid of a partnership and a corporation.

368. D. OWBPA (the Older Workers Benefit Protection Act) is an amendment to the Age Discrimination in Employment Act (ADEA). This OWBPA establishes conditions under which an employer can offer employees incentives to retire early while asking them to waive their right to sue the company for additional benefits. These conditions include clearly written agreements, providing something of value beyond what the employee is already entitled to and a reminder that they should consult with an attorney before signing a release.

369. B. Quid pro quo literally means, "this for that". It is a term used to indicate sexual harassment where a supervisor requires sexual favors in exchange for a favourable Tangible Employment Action (TEA).

370. C. The Worker Adjustment and Retraining Notification Act (WARN Act) requires employers with 100 or more full time employees to provide 60 calendar-day advance notification of plant closings and mass layoffs

of employees. However, a plant closing is defined as when 50 or more full-time employees lose their jobs a single plant shuts down.

371. D. The EEOC sets out guidelines for the prevention of sexual harassment stating that employers are encouraged to implement options A,B, C.

372. C. A divestiture is the reduction of an asset or business through sale, liquidation, exchange, closure, or any other means for financial or ethical reasons. The Minks Inc. plans to divest the car sales company. Divestiture is the opposite of investment.

373. C. As stated, sustainability seeks to meet the needs of the present without compromising the ability of future generations to meet their own needs.

374. A. In a Management By Objective process, goals are generally set by the central management and then diffused to divisional and departmental objectives,goals are not bottom-up but Top-down in a MBO.

375. D. A HR Audit is a comprehensive method of reviewing current human resources policies, procedures, documentation and systems to identify needs for improvement of the HR function as well as to assess compliance with laws, rules and regulations.

376. A. The Americans with Disabilities Act (ADA) requires employers to reasonably accommodate employees with disabilities. Leave is one accommodation that may be considered reasonable, even if an employee needs more leave than allowed by company policy. In this case, the best option is to reinstate the employee and accommodate the therapy sessions by modifying the employee's work hours.

377. B. The Rehabilitation Act of 1973, was put in place to correct the problem of discrimination against people with disabilities in the United States.

378. B. Title VII prohibits employers from treating or hiring applicants or employees differently because of their membership in a protected class such as race or sex, this is known as disparate treatment.

379. A. The FMLA entitles eligible employees of covered employers to take unpaid, job-protected leave for specified family and medical reasons with continuation of group health insurance coverage under the same terms and conditions as if the employee had not taken leave. It covers employers with 50 employees within a 75 mile radius.

380. B. The FLSA states that willful violations may be prosecuted criminally and the violator fined up to $10,000. Employers who wilfully or repeatedly violate the minimum wage or overtime pay requirements are subject to a civil money penalty of up to $1,100 for each violation.

381. D. A claim of Negligent Hiring will allege that if the employer had engaged in more due diligence when screening the worker, a history of violent or prohibitive conduct would have been revealed which should have disqualified the worker from consideration. Reference and background checks help to avoid negligent hiring claims.

382. A. A job is a group of homogeneous tasks related by similarity of functions; this consists of duties, responsibilities, and tasks.

383. B. OSHA states that any employer who willfully or repeatedly violates the requirements of the Act may be assessed a civil penalty of not more than $70,000 for each violation, but not less than $5,000 for each willful violation.

384. B. Variable pay is an incentive or bonus employers pay to employees whose performance meets or exceeds company expectations, provided the company meets its own goals for productivity and profitability. It is subject to change and option B is correct.

385. D. Union deauthorization is a formal process employees use to remove a union security clause. The National Labor Relations Board (NLRB) specifies rules for deauthorization and decertification (which means to end union representation) elections. One such rule is that a deauthorization petition must be signed by 30 percent of the members of the bargaining unit. In this case just 20% of employees have signed the petition. Therefore, the NLRB must deny the petition.

386. C. Criterion validity assesses whether a test reflects a certain set of abilities therefore criterion validity is established when the test predicts or correlates the behavior. Criterion validity is often divided into concurrent and predictive validity.

387. D. The Civil Rights Act of 1991 expanded coverage to include international employees of American businesses unless compliance will violate the laws of the host country; Race norming which means modifying employment related tests on the basis of race or ethnicity became illegal; the Act limited the rights of non-parties to attack consent decrees which is an agreement or settlement to resolve a dispute between two parties without admission of guilt or liability.

388. B. Employee evaluation is a synonym for performance appraisal. Paired comparison and 360 degree feedback are methods of performance appraisals not synonyms.

389. A. A correlation coefficient is a statistical measure of the degree to which changes to the value of one variable predict change to the value of another variable.

390. A. A no-solicitation policy can be used to prevent union organizing in the workplace as long as other non-employees and outside groups are similarly prevented from solicitation including selling candy bars to raise funds.

391. C. An alternative work schedule permits a variation from the employee's core hours in starting and departure times, but does not alter the total number of hours worked in a week. Job sharing is an alternative work schedule where typically two people are retained on a part-time or reduced-time basis to perform a job normally fulfilled by one person working full-time.

392. C. Title VII of the Civil Rights Act protects employees from religious discrimination and requires employers to reasonably accommodate an employee's religious beliefs or practices unless doing so would cause an undue hardship. Denying the request without exploring other options is therefore inappropriate since the law requires the employer's involvement in the accommodation process. The best course of action is for the employer to see if other employees can swap work days to accommodate this employee's beliefs.

393. B. Job analysis is the process of gathering and analyzing information about the content, requirements of jobs and the context in which jobs are performed. This process is used to determine job descriptions, job specifications and placement of jobs.

394. A. The Americans with Disabilities Act (ADA), the Family and Medical Leave Act (FMLA) and workers' compensation are all laws that provide some level of protection for employees whose illness or injury interferes with their ability to work. Since the provisions of the laws can overlap depending on the circumstances, and the intent is to protect employee rights, the correct answer is to follow the law that is most beneficial to the employee.

395. C. Performance Appraisal is the systematic evaluation of the performance of employees to understand the abilities of a person for further growth and development.

396. B. Cost per Hire = (Total External Costs) + (Total Internal Costs) / Total Number of Hires. The answer is Option B.

397. D. Change management is a systematic approach to dealing with change both from the perspective of an organization and the individual. Some characteristics of change include option A, B and C.

398. **B.** *The EEOC enforces anti-discrimination laws that give a limited amount of time to file a charge of discrimination (also called statute of limitation), the charge is to be filed within 180 calendar days from the day the discrimination took place. The 180 calendar day filing deadline is extended to 300 calendar days if a state or local agency enforces a law that prohibits employment discrimination on the same basis.*

399. **C.** *HR forecasting is a process that helps to determine how many employees a company will need in the future to meet its strategic goals; it involves establishing what jobs the company will need to fill, what types of skills are required and what challenges the company will face in meeting its staffing needs. This is different from a job analysis which is a process to identify the job duties and determine the importance of these duties for a given job.*

400. **C.** *The correct answer is option C. The case established that the complainant in an employment discrimination lawsuit carries the initial burden to present a prima facie case for racial discrimination.*

Section 5 Questions

401. The limit on the amount of compensatory and punitive damages a person can recover from an employer with 435 employees is?
a. $50,000.
b. $150,000.
c. $200,000.
d. $300,000.

402. Suggestion programs, town meetings, and opinion surveys best foster:
a. Electronic communication.
b. Upward communication.
c. Union organizing.
d. Employee performance.

403. Is Tim protected by the Age Discrimination in Employment Act (ADEA) even though he is 39 years old?
a. Yes, any employee who is being discriminated against on the basis of age is protected.
b. Yes, Reverse discrimination is protected under ADEA.
c. No, the ADEA protects individuals from the age of 40 and above.
d. None of the above.

404. A workers' compensation injury would not be OSHA recordable if the injury:
a. Was caused by no specific accident.
b. Occurred when an employee fell in a parking lot and received first aid treatment.
c. Resulted from an equipment malfunction.
d. Resulted from the violation of an established safety rule.

405. The job characteristics model as designed by Hackman and Oldham are?
a. Skill variety, task identity, task significance, autonomy, and feedback.
b. Strategy, goal and objective.
c. Motivation and incentives.
d. Job analysis, Job description and Job evaluation.

406. Which of the following is not a way that a company can set up its departments?
a. Divisional.
b. Functional.
c. Product.

d. Structural.

407. The most effective way to prevent workplace violence is to:
a. Providing workers' compensation.
b. Have a zero-tolerance policy regarding violence in the workplace.
c. Establish an employee assistance program.
d. Use background checks to determine if the potential employee has a history of violence.

408. The ADA prohibits which of the following?
a. An employer makes a pre-employment inquiry in an interview as to whether an individual is disabled.
b. An employer asks a job applicant whether he or she can perform particular job functions.
c. An employer selects the most qualified applicant over a candidate with a disability.
d. None of the above.

409. Under OSHA standards, which of the following procedures is required of each employee in a lockout/tagout program?
a. Equipment disabling.
b. Hazard management reports.
c. Formal annual training.
d. Lockout license.

410. Tina is claims she is discriminated against because she has a known relationship with a disabled colleague. Does Tina's claims have any basis?
a. No, the ADA only protects individuals with disabilities.
b. No, the ADA does not apply to employees who do not have disabilities themselves.
c. Yes, the ADA protects persons discriminated against because they have a known association or relationship with a disabled individual.
d. Tina is protected under the Rehabilitation Act but not under the ADA.

411. Which of the following is not an OSHA violation?
a. Other-than-serious.
b. Failure to abate.
c. De-maximus.
d. Repeat.

412. A software engineer at a coding company has brought in medical documentation indicating an inability to perform the essential functions of the position due to medical reasons. What action should the employer take first?
a. Consult with the EAP provider.
b. Create an approximate role of accommodation in terms of status and pay.
c. Terminate the employee for creating an undue hardship.
d. Review the medical documentation against the essential job functions.

413. OSHA's primary goal is?
a. Issuing citations.
b. Correcting hazards and maintaining compliance.
c. Collecting penalties.
d. Ensuring diversity of safety communication.

414. OSHA compliance safety and health officer must do which of the following when visiting a company for an inspection?
a. Issue a citation.
b. Give advanced notice to the employer.
c. Explain why the organization has been targeted for inspection.
d. Obtain an inspection warrant.

415. Disparate impact means?
a. when a women is required to take tests that men are not required to.
b. When an Asian is assumed to be smarter than an Hispanic.
c. Seemingly fair practices that have an adverse effect on a protected class.
d. The legal right to ask an employee to resign, with or without reason.

416. Which of the following is true about the following labor legislations;
a. Sherman Antitrust Act of 1890 - It allowed injunctions to forbid groups that conspired to restrain trade.
b. Norris-La Guardia Act of 1932 - protected the rights of workers to organize without the interference of federal injunctions.
c. NLRA or Wagner Act of 1935 - identified the 5 employer unfair labor practices.
d. All of the above.

417. The following are performance review methods except;
a. Educational.
b. Narrative.
c. Rating.
d. Comparison.

418. HR risks can be classified in the following areas except;
a. Legal and Compliance.
b. Security.
c. Workplace monitoring.
d. Business continuity.

419. The Drug-Free Workplace Act of 1970 applies to businesses with federal contracts of $100,000 or more each year. What is inaccurate in this statement?
a. The Act was established for state contractors not federal contractors.
b. The Act was established in 1988 not 1970.
c. The entire statement is accurate.
d. The Act applies to businesses with federal contracts worth $50,000.

420. The Labor-Management Relations Act (LMRA) of 1947 established the following except;
a. It gave employees the right to sue the union.
b. The LMRA prohibits closed shops and allows union shops only with the consent of employee majority.

c. It prohibited jurisdictional strikes and secondary boycotts.
d. The LMRA allows employers to permanently replace striking union workers.

421. Which of the following is considered a business continuity risk?
a. Environmental disasters.
b. Organized disruptions.
c. Hacking of business information systems.
d. All of the above

422. The following are unlawful activities that could pose a HR risk to an organisation with regard to legal compliance except;
a. Discrimination.
b. Understaffing.
c. Sexual harassment.
d. Negligent hiring.

423. HR risks with regard to workplace privacy include which of the following;
a. Identity theft.
b. Natural disaster.
c. Priority disruptions.
d. Hardware malfunction.

424. A bell curve ranking method means;
a. Rating a small group of employees at a high scale, a small group at the bottom scale and the majority at an average scale.
b. Rating a large group of employees both at the top and bottom, with a small number of employees at the average scale.
c. Rating employees as low as possible.
d. Rating employees as high as possible.

425. Which of the following is NOT a HR risk with regard to Safety and Health?
a. Ergonomic strains.
b. Repetitive stress injuries.
c. System failures.
d. Workplace injuries

426. All of these are true about an HR audit except;
a. It determines the HR practices to continue or discontinue.
b. It is a key means of measuring HR effectiveness.
c. It positions HR as a business partner.
d. It is not effective when outsourced.

427. The HR tools used to identify and assess risks are?
a. Workplace investigation.
b. HR Audits.

c. HR Risk management.
d. A and B.

428. The union at ANAT company wants to receive automatic deductions as union dues. To be enforceable, what must happen?
a. The union must get permission from the NLRB.
b. The union must get permission from the employees.
c. The employees must give written authorization for the deductions.
d. Members of the union agree to deductions when they decide to have a union.

429. An HR audit in the compensation and benefits functional area will NOT assess which of the following;
a. Structure of the HR department.
b. Consistency of compensation philosophy.
c. Wage compression.
d. Health-care cost review.

430. A totality of agreement means;
a. A zipper clause.
b. A clause which states that the CBA is the entire agreement between the parties.
c. A and B.
d. A reform of the LMRA.

431. Secondary boycotts were declared illegal by which of the following?
a. Taft-Hartley Act.
b. Clayton Act.
c. Wagner Act.
d. Landrum Griffith Act.

432. The TIE company is conducting an HR audit of the Employee Relations department only. What is likely to be assessed?
a. Conflict-resolution processes.
b. Turnover demographics.
c. Diversity practices.
d. All of the above.

433. Which of the following can be subject to implied contracts if not properly documented?
a. Employee Handbooks.
b. Employment Contracts.
c. Employee Intranet.
d. All of the above.

434. Which of the following acts deals directly with discrimination in compensation?

a. Service Contract Act.
b. Pay Equity.
c. Fair Labor Standards Act.
d. Equal Pay Act.

435. Which of the following is incorrect with regard to the TIPS acronym in labor relations?
a. Threaten.
b. Inform.
c. Promise.
d. Spy.

436. A voluntary benefit offered to employees who lose their jobs is called?
a. COBRA.
b. Unemployment compensation.
c. Severance pay.
d. Workers compensation.

437. Pay that is consistent in each pay period despite the number of hours worked is?
a. Incentives.
b. Wages.
c. Salary.
d. Differential pay.

438. Which of the following determines if the NLRB will consider an acquiring owner to be a successor employer?
a. Substantial continuity of operations.
b. Similarity of operations and products.
c. All of the above.
d. None of the above.

439. An HR audit focused only on recruitment practices, affirmative action programs and labor market demographics is most likely on which of these functional areas;
a. Organization of HR Function.
b. Labor relations.
c. HR Risk management.
d. Workforce planning and employment.

440. Which of the following is not not a major factor in establishing compensation within an organization?
a. IRS rules.
b. Labor market conditions.
c. Employee salary history.
d. Company competition salary survey.

441. The following are true about the work stoppages listed below except;
a. Lockouts- when management shuts down operations.
b. Boycotts-when management avoids negotiations.
c. Strikes- when the union decides to stop working.

d. All of the above.

442. What is the name of the act that defines what is included as hours worked and is therefore compensable and a factor in calculating overtime?
a. Equal Pay Act.
b. McNamara O'Hara Act.
c. Davis Bacon Act.
d. Portal-to-Portal Act.

443. Why should an HR audit focus on pre-employment tests?
a. To ensure the tests are valid and reliable.
b. To abide by the Uniform Guidelines on Employee Selection Procedures.
c. A and B only.
d. To determine if alternative staffing methods are required.

444. The Tinge company have had extensive analysis on employee benefits which they believe should be presented as a bill to Congress, what is the first step the Tinge company should take?
a. Submit the idea to the Senate for review.
b. Submit the idea to the House of Representative for review.
c. Submit the idea to a representative from the congressional district.
d. None of the above.

445. An unlawful strike in which employees stop working and stay in the building is called;
a. Sit-down strike.
b. Work stoppage.
c. Economic strike.
d. Work slowdown.

446. Contractors must do the following to be in compliance with the Drug-Free Workplace Act of 1988 except;
a. Develop a written policy stating they provide a drug-free workplace.
b. Develop a program to educate employees about the dangers of drug abuse.
c. Establish penalties for illegal drug convictions.
d. Train employees on proper use of equipment.

447. Which of the following forms of application is best for internal recruitment?
a. Weighted application.
b. Short-form application.
c. Long-form application.
d. Job-specific application.

448. Mark Harris owns two companies, one is unionized, the other is not unionized. This can be referred to as;
a. Secondary boycott.
b. Alter Ego doctrine.
c. Double-breasting.

d. Ally doctrine.

449. What is the significance of the Health Insurance Portability and Accountability Act (HIPAA) ?
a. Ensure health coverage for retired employees.
b. To protect employees covered under COBRA.
c. Prohibit discrimination based on pre-existing health problems or conditions.
d. All of the above.

450. The Occupational Safety and Health Act (OSHA) established 3 duties for the workplace, which of the following is not one of them?
a. Employers must provide a workplace free from recognized hazards.
b. Employers must research and evaluate workplace hazards.
c. Employers must comply with all safety and health standards.
d. Employees must comply with occupational safety and health standards.

451. The Drug-Free Workplace Act of 1988 applies to which of the following?
a. Government agencies.
b. Federal contractors.
c. Universities.
d. All of the above.

452. When an employer whose workers are on strike contacts a neutral employer to perform the work of the striking workers, this can be referred to as;
a. Alter Ego doctrine.
b. Ally doctrine.
c. LMRA boycotts.
d. Unfair Labor Practice.

453. What seating style is best for a training that will involve a wide range of activities such as lectures, filming, group work and individual presentations?
a. Classroom-style.
b. Chevron-style.
c. Theater-style.
d. U-shaped style

454. When an employer has two businesses with substantially identical management, operations and ownership, this is known as;
a. Alter Ego employer.
b. Ally employer.
c. Double-breasting.
d. Mediation.

455. Which of the following pieces of legislation establishes guidelines for retaining and reporting employee identification records?
a. Personal Responsibility & Work Opportunity Reconciliation Act.
b. Fair Credit Reporting Act.
c. Family Medical Leave Act.

d. Consumer Credit Protection Act.

456. The HR Manager of the GRIT company is concerned as a company whose operations complements the that of the GRIT company is suffering a strike by its union. The GRIT company is involved in;
a. Straight-line operations.
b. Boycotting.
c. Yellow-dog contracts.
d. Contract clauses.

457. A workplace condition described as "harmful physical and emotional responses that occur when the requirements of the job do not match the capabilities, resources, or needs of the worker." is most likely?
a. Violence.
b. Stress.
c. Tension.
d. Incompetence.

458. Which of the following refers to the ability to determine how much of a product or service can be produced?
a. Production Layout.
b. Capacity.
c. Equipment.
d. Weighted average.

459. The HR Manager of YET company recently informed the union members that secondary boycotts are ULPs. What is a secondary boycott?
a. When a union intends to go on strike.
b. When a union intends to picket.
c. When a union tries to compel an employer to stop doing business with an employer the union has a dispute with.
d. None of the above.

460. Which of the following refers to ensuring a product or service attains the required standard?
a. Cost control.
b. Quality assurance.
c. Inventory control.
d. Scheduling.

461. What is a wildcat strike?
a. A strike in response to a ULP violation.
b. Unannounced industrial action in violation of a contract clause prohibiting strikes.
c. A strike in support of a hot-cargo clause.
d. A strike against a hot-cargo clause.

462. Which of the following questions is irrelevant in strategic planning?

a. Where are we now?
b. Where are we coming from?
c. Where do we want to be?
d. How will we know when we arrive?

463. The Labor Management Reporting and Disclosure Act (LMRDA) of 1959 established which of the following;
a. It placed controls on internal union operations.
b. It restricted increases in union dues and extortionate picketing.
c. It provides safeguards against retaliatory disciplinary actions by the union.
d. All of the above.

464. Which of these is the most important reason why performance evaluations should be documented?
a. To ensure employees perform their duties as at when due.
b. To serve as a structures means of communication.
c. To help defend employment actions, positive or negative.
d. To provide performance feedback.

465. The REEG company's union has embarked on a strike to obtain better pay and working conditions, this strike is;
a. Unlawful and economic.
b. Lawful and economic.
c. An unfair labor practices.
d. AN NLRB infraction.

466. Discriminatory hiring actions can be allowed under Title VII in which case;
a. Fiduciary Basis.
b. Discriminatory hiring actions are not allowed under Title VII
c. Influence on corporate leadership
d. Bona fide Occupational Qualifications (BFOQ)

467. The following makes a strike unlawful except?
a. If it occurs in response to an employer unfair labor practice.
b. If it supports union unfair labor practices.
c. If the strikers engage in serious misconduct.
d. If it violates a no-strike clause in the contract.

468. Ann is frustrated because her supervisor always rates the entire team in a specific band at the middle of the rating scale. Ann's supervisor is most likely using what rater error?
a. Leniency.
b. Central tendency.
c. Knowledge of predictor.
d. All of the above.

469. A best practice in performance appraisal is;

a. For supervisors to provide constant feedback to employees.
b. Communicate performance expectations clearly.
c. Set goals for the next review period.
d. All of the above.

470. The CEO of LIN INC has informed employees that joining a union may hinder promotion chances. This is an example of;
a. Interference.
b. Intimidation.
c. Unfair Labor Practices.
d. Prohibitive activities.

471. An example of lobbying is;
a. A member of congress sponsors a bill
b. A non-profit organisation finds a sponsor for a bill.
c. A congress committee conducts an approval for a bill.
d. A senator seeks presidential backing on a bill.

472. In the case of Stender v. Lucky Stores, which of these is true;
a. The HR team were found culpable of negligent hiring.
b. A lawsuit on gender discrimination was filed following information from a diversity training.
c. A lawsuit on repatriation of non-US citizens.
d. Flexible work arrangements were found to be discriminatory.

473. The acronym TIPS helps to make sure employers avoid prohibited labor activity. What does TIPS stand for?
a. Threaten, Indict, Promise and Spy on employees.
b. Threaten, Interrogate, Promise or Spy on employees.
c. Threaten, Interrogate, Propagate and Spy on employees.
d. Threaten, Investigate, Promise or Spy on employees.

474. The Rehabilitation Act of 1973 pertains to all these except;
a. Prohibits discrimination on the basis of disability in programs run by all agencies.
b. Covers federal contractors with contracts of $10,000+.
c. Requires federal information technology to be accessible to people with disabilities.
d. Prohibits federal employers from discriminating against qualified people with disabilities.

475. Employers must not enter into a hot-cargo agreement. What is a hot-cargo agreement?
a. An importation clause.
b. Union organizing.
c. When at the union's request, employers stop doing business with another employer.
d. Refusing to bargain in good faith.

476. The following are crucial to an effective repatriation program except;
a. Assistance in managing the transition to and from the host country.
b. Effective repatriate knowledge management.
c. Provide employment for the employee's spouse.
d. One-on-one debrief between the manager and repatriate.

477. Featherbedding is a ULP, what does it mean?
a. When unions require employers to keep employees on jobs rendered obsolete by technology.
b. Restrain manager's ability to discipline union members.
c. Turn a blind eye to union excessive dues and membership fees.
d. Featherbedding is a legal term for administrative law court corruption.

478. The RTT corporation is being investigated for discriminatory promotion practices. The company HRIS will be helpful to;
a. Provide trends and ratio analyses of the company's promotion processes.
b. Provide data related to the corporation's affirmative action processes and performance evaluations.
c. Provide summary comparison of promotion forecast.
d. Provide data on the EEO-1 and OFCCP compliance forms.

479. In which of these instances is picketing unlawful?
a. When another union has been lawfully recognized as the bargaining representative.
b. When a representation election was held within the previous 12 months.
c. When a representation election is not filed within 30 days of the start of the picketing.
d. All of the above.

480. Job reinforcement is critical to;
a. Effective transfer of training.
b. Supervisory authority.
c. Negative accelerating curve.
d. Change increments.

481. Yellow dog contracts entails which of the following?
a. Employers used yellow-dog contracts to prevent employees from joining unions by signing agreements.
b. The agreement stipulates that joining a union in the future will be sufficient grounds for dismissal.
c. A and B.
d. None of the above.

482. The ADAAA defined disability as an impairment that substantially limits one or more major life activities. The following are correct under the ADAAA except;

a. Specified that disability includes any impairment that is in remission if it will substantially limit a life activity when active.
b. Reasonable accommodation must be provided for current illegal users of drugs.
c. Prohibits consideration of ameliorative effects of mitigating measures when assessing an impairment.
d. Major life activities is expanded to include major bodily functions.

483. The following are NLRB remedies when an Employer engages in ULPs except?
a. Disband an employer-dominated union.
b. Engage in the collective bargaining process.
c. Change company ownership.
d. Reinstate employees to positions held prior to the ULP.

484. What is the training cost for each employee in this scenario; $5,000 was spent for the training, $1,000 for the training location; 30 full-time employees (40 hours/week) and 4 part-time employees (20 hours/week).
a. $200.
b. $187.50
c. $155.50.
d. $147.50.

485. The following are NLRB remedies when a Union engages in ULPs except?
a. Refund excessive dues with interest to members.
b. Engage in the collective bargaining process.
c. Sign a written agreement with the employer.
d. Disband the union.

486. Company TIC has embarked on a survey on customer satisfaction with their detergent range. This survey was sent to 3,000 of the current estimate of 5,000 customers. Company TIC is using;
a. A sample.
b. A distribution.
c. A prerequisite population
d. The top customers.

487. ULPs must be filed to the NLRB within what timeframe of the incident?
a. 30 days.
b. 6 months.
c. Immediately the incident occurred.
d. 9 months.

488. Monetary compensation includes the following except;
a. 401(k) matching.
b. Pension plans.
c. Employee Stock Ownership Programs (ESOPs).

d. Intrinsic rewards.

489. Groups of employees strongly challenge supervisors about benefits and employment practices. What is likely happening?
a. Picketing.
b. Union organizing.
c. Impending strike.
d. NLRB elections.

490. The Age Discrimination in Employment Act of 1967 (ADEA) stipulates the following except;
a. The ADEA overrides the procedures of hiring of firefighters and police officers.
b. Prohibits discrimination against persons 40 years of age or older.
c. The ADEA applies to businesses with more than 20 employees.
d. Waiver of rights must include a period of 21 days to review the waiver.

491. Which of these is not a part of the union recognition process?
a. Signing of authorization cards.
b. Demand for recognition.
c. Petition to LMRA for elections.
d. Election.

492. Non-monetary compensation includes the following except;
a. Telecommuting.
b. Flex-time.
c. Recognition.
d. Direct compensation.

493. The NLRB will hold an election if ----- show support for the petition?
a. 30% of the eligible employees.
b. 50% of the eligible employees.
c. 25% of the eligible employees.
d. 31% of all employees.

494. The following will be assessed in an HR audit except;
a. Strategic planning.
b. Benefits and compensation.
c. FLSA compliance.
d. HRIS system.

495. Wayne, the HR Supervisor has agreed to a neutrality agreement with the union before realizing he is not sure what it means? Can you help Wayne?
a. It means the employer has agreed to a NLRB election.
b. It means the employer has agreed not to say or do anything in opposition to the union.
c. It means the employer is neutral to union ULPs.
d. None of the above.

496. Any employee benefit not associated with wages and salaries is known as;
a. Non-monetary compensation.
b. Social Society benefits.
c. Indirect compensation.
d. Internal payments.

497. When an employer agrees to recognize a union based on signed authorization cards, this is called?
a. Easy recognition.
b. Unionization.
c. Black-dog agreements.
d. Card-check election.

498. Which of the following is correct under the ADEA?
a. Waivers of rights and waivers involving exits have the same considerations.
b. The ADEA protects against discharge or discipline for just cause.
c. Waivers on exits or termination require 45 days to consider the agreement.
d. ADEA does not provide for BFOQs to the business operations.

499. The NLRB in devising a bargaining unit seeks to determine if there is a "community of interest" in the unit. What does this mean?
a. To ensure the interests of the unit members are sufficiently similar.
b. To ensure the unit is not a fictional arrangement.
c. To ensure bickerings do not ensue.
d. None of the above.

500. Which of these is an important aspect of a Total Rewards Program?
a. Differentiating jobs.
b. Business risks.
c. Managerial constraints.
d. An annual bonus.

Section 5 Answers and Explanations

401. C. *The EEOC places limits on the amount of compensatory and punitive damages a person can recover. These limits vary depending on the size of the employer; For employers with 15-100 employees, the limit is $50,000; For employers with 101-200 employees, the limit is $100,000; For employers with 201-500 employees, the limit is $200,000 and For employers with more than 500 employees, the limit is $300,000.*

402. B. *Suggestion programs give employees the opportunity to submit ideas for improving an organization's operations to management. Town meetings are large group meetings where a senior leader of an organization provides updates and gives employees the opportunity to ask questions. Opinion surveys are anonymous tools used to ask employees how they feel about their jobs and the organization. All of these tools encourage employees to communicate upward to management as Upward communication are questions, inquiries and complaints that employees direct toward their superiors.*

403. C. *The Age Discrimination in Employment Act (ADEA) protects only employees and job applicants who are 40 years of age or older. The ADEA does not permit reverse age discrimination claims.*

404. **B.** The Occupational Safety and Health Act (OSHA) requires covered employers to record work-related injuries and illnesses. This includes injuries and illnesses that result in death, days away from work, restricted work or transfer to another job, loss of consciousness and medical treatment beyond first aid. Option B is minor and requires only first aid.

405. **A.** The job characteristics model, designed by Hackman and Oldham, is based on the idea that a challenging job enhances motivation, there are five core job characteristics (skill variety, task identity, task significance, autonomy, and feedback).

406. **D.** Organizations can set up departments based on functional, product-based, geographic, divisional and matrix structures, structural departments is not a valid option.

407. **D.** The most effective way to prevent workplace violence is to make every effort to prevent potentially violent individuals from being hired. Screening candidates for convictions for violent crimes, for example, can help prevent violence early on.

408. **A.** Under the ADA, an employer may not make a pre-employment inquiry on an application form or in an interview as to whether, or to what extent, an individual is disabled.

409. **C.** OSHA requires lockout/tagout procedures that are designed to make sure that equipment is turned off and safe to be around while performing repairs and maintenance. Licensing is not required but formal training is. Inspections are also required but they need to be conducted at least annually.

410. **C.** The ADA states that employment discrimination is prohibited against qualified individuals with disabilities. As well as persons discriminated against because they have a known association or relationship with a disabled individual.

411. **C.** OSHA violations are categorized as willful, serious, other-than-serious, de minimis, failure to abate, and repeated. De-maximus is not an OSHA violation.

412. **D.** The Americans with Disabilities Act (ADA) requires employers to reasonably accommodate employees with disabilities so that they can perform the essential functions of their job. The employee's medical documentation suggests that they cannot perform the essential functions but efore the employer terminates the employee, the employer should compare the medical documentation to the job's essential functions. Employers are not required to create positions for employees in situations like these.

413. **B.** OSHA's primary goal is correcting hazards and maintaining compliance not issuing citations or collecting penalties.

414. **C.** OSHA (the Occupational Safety and Health Administration) inspectors, called compliance safety and health officers are to assure compliance with OSHA requirements and help employers and workers reduce on-the-job hazards and prevent injuries, illnesses and deaths in the workplace. After presenting their credentials, the compliance officer will hold an opening conference with the employer in which they will explain why the organisation was selected for inspection and what the inspection will involve. The employer is expected to provide a representative to participate in the inspection. OSHA must issue a citation and proposed penalty -- if any -- within six months of the violation not during the inspection.

415. **C.** Under Title VII of the Civil Rights Act of 1964, disparate impact is a seemingly neutral employment practice that does not appear to be discriminatory on face value but discriminatory in its application or effect.

416. **D.** The options are all true, also the Norris-La Guardia Act outlawed yellow-dog contracts (contracts employers used to prevent employees from joining a union); the NLRA also created the NLRB.

417. **A.** The performance review methods are narrative, rating, comparison and behavioral. There is no educational performance review method.

418. C. *HR Risks can be classified into 5 areas; Legal and compliance; Safety and health; Security; Business continuity and Workplace privacy. Workplace monitoring is not a HR Risk Classification.*

419. B. *The inaccurate portion is the year, the Drug-Free Workplace Act was established in 1988 not 1970.*

420. A. *The LMRA also called the Taft-Hartley Act prohibited unions from charging excessive dues and from "featherbedding," but it was the Labor Management Reporting and Disclosure Act (LMRDA) of 1959 that gave employees the right to sue the union.*

421. D. *Business continuity risks include option A, B and C as well as disruption of public services such as power outages.*

422. B. *Understaffing may result in lower productivity and stress but is not illegal.*

423. A. *Only Identity Theft is clearly a workplace privacy risk.*

424. A. *A bell-curve is a performance evaluation process which rewards a small percentage of top performers, encourages a large majority in the middle to improve, and lays-off the bottom performers.*

425. C. *System or equipment failures are a risk to business continuity not to Health and Safety.*

426. D. *HR Audits are actually more effective when outsourced, there is greater accuracy and objectivity.*

427. D. *HR Audits and Workplace investigations are used to identify and assess risks.*

428. C. *Dues Check-off means a voluntarily authorized and regular deduction of an employee's wages by an employer to pay off the union dues. An employee must give written authorization for a dues check-off.*

429. A. *An HR audit in the <u>Organization of HR function area</u> will assess the structure of the HR department. The compensation and benefit area audit will handle areas that deal with rewards, pay and benefits.*

430. C. *A totality of agreement represents the full and entire agreement between both parties who waive the right to demand bargaining on any matter not dealt with in the contract, regardless of whether that matter was contemplated when the contract was negotiated or signed. It is also called a zipper clause.*

431. A. *The Taft-Hartley Act also called the Labor Management Relations Act prohibited closed shops, jurisdictional strikes and secondary boycotts.*

432. D. *Option A, B and C are all aspects of Employee Relations.*

433. A. *Employee handbook explains company policies and benefits, disciplinary procedures and if not properly written, may leave room for implied meanings.*

434. D. *The Equal Pay Act of 1963 amended the Fair Labor Standards Act to abolish wage discrimination based on sex.*

435. B. *The TIPS acronym states that employers may not threaten, <u>interrogate</u>, promise or spy on employees. TIPS are Unfair Labor Practices (ULP).*

436. C. *Of all the options, only the severance pay is voluntary.*

437. C. *A salary is paid as a fixed amount per pay period regardless of hours worked (exempt) and while wages are paid by the hour (non-exempt).*

438. C. When a company with Collective Bargaining Agreements (CBA) is acquired, the new company may be required to maintain the CBAs. The NLRB will consider the new company as a successor employer when there is a significant continuity and similarity of operations; the number of employees absorbed into the new company and the agreement with the previous employer.

439. D. Workforce planning involves workforce supply analysis, demand analysis, gap analysis and strategy development. Recruitment, affirmative action and labor market demographics are in line with workforce planning.

440. C. In establishing employee compensation, employee salary history is not a major factor in establishing the process.

441. B. A boycott is a practice utilized in labor disputes whereby an organized group of employees refrain from dealing with an employer. A "secondary" boycott - boycotts those who do business with the primary target of the boycotters, it is an unfair labor practice under Federal law.

442. D. The Portal to Portal Act of 1947 was an amendment to the FLSA, it defined compensable work time which is a factor in calculating overtime.

443. C. Pre-employment testing are to abide by option A and B; tests should not have a disparate impact on the basis of race, color, religion, sex, or national origin and must be job-related and consistent with business necessity.

444. C. When an idea for a bill originates from an individual or business outside of Congress, the idea must first be submitted to a member of Congress (known as MOC). This MOC may be either a senator or a representative. The MOC will then sponsor the bill by submitting it to the part of Congress where he or she works, and the bill will begin its journey through legislation.

445. A. A sitdown strike is illegal and occurs when strikers refuse to leave the employer's premises.

446. D. The Occupational Safety and Health Act (OSHA) requires employers to provide a workplace free of known hazards and to train employees on proper use of equipment not the Drug-Free Workplace Act.

447. B. Internal recruitment will require minimal information as it pertains to current employees for which the company already has the employee's information on file and will require only a formal application rather than a detailed application form as will be necessary for an external candidate.

448. C. Double-breasting occurs when there is a common owner of a unionized business and a non-unionized business.

449. C. The Health Insurance Portability and Accountability Act (HIPAA) improves the portability and continuity of health insurance coverage, it prohibits health benefit discrimination toward employees based on pre-existing health conditions. HIPAA also safeguards Protected Health Information (PHI).

450. B. National Institute for Occupational Safety and Health (NIOSH) is the federal agency responsible for conducting research and making recommendations for the prevention of work-related injury and illness, this is not the responsibility of the OSHA administration or employers.

451. B. The Drug-Free Workplace Act of 1988 applies specifically to federal contractors with federal contracts of $100,000 and above.

452. B. The term described is the ally doctrine.

453. B. The chevron-style seating (V shaped) is best for training activities that involve several activities as it is versatile and can accommodate varieties of group activities.

454. A. The term described is an Alter Ego employer.

455. A. The Personal Responsibility and Work Opportunity Reconciliation Act of 1996 establishes and updates rules for retaining and reporting employee identification records.

456. A. Straight-line operations occur when two businesses perform complementary operations.

457. B. According to The National Institute of Occupational Safety and Health (NIOSH), the above is the definition of stress that affects employees in the workplace.

458. B. Capacity is the maximum output that a business can produce in a given period with the available resources.

459. C. A secondary boycott is an industrial action by a union against a company on the grounds that it does business with another company engaged in a labor dispute.

460. B. Quality assurance refers to the maintenance of a desired level of quality in a service or product, especially by giving attention to every stage of the process of production and delivery.

461. B. A wildcat strike which is spontaneous or unannounced illegal industrial action by a section of employees, without following the proper procedure for striking.

462. B. It is irrelevant to analyze the past when planning strategies for the present. The company's present state should be analysed (where are we now?) and onwards.

463. D. The LMRDA established option A,B and C. It also established a Bill of Rights for union members; reporting requirements for labor organizations; standards for the regular election of union officers; and safeguards for protecting labor organization funds.

464. C. Performance evaluations have a significant impact on salary administration, performance feedback, promotions and training. These significant employment actions require documentation above all else, to identify the basis upon which they were taken.

465. B. Economic strikes are embarked upon to obtain some economic gain such as higher wages, shorter hours or improved working conditions. Economic strikers retain their statuses as employees because the employer cannot discharge them but can replace them.

466. D. A BFOQ is a work requirement reasonably necessary to the normal performance of a job, such as being a certain age or gender, or having the ability to lift a certain amount of weight. BFOQ in good faith can be legal such as being female to work as a fitter in a lingerie department.

467. A. Employees who strike to protest an unfair labor practice committed by their employer can neither be discharged nor permanently replaced. ULP strikes are legal. Employer ULPs include interference with union activities, discrimination against an employee for filing charges with the NLRB or refusal to bargain with a lawful union

468. B. The Central tendency bias refers to a tendency for supervisors to evaluate most of their employees as "average" on a rating scale.

469. D. Option A,B,C are best practices in performance appraisal as well as documentation of performance evaluation.

470. C. Employer ULPs include Threats, Interference, Promises, Spying or Interrogations. The CEO has issued a threat which is a ULP.

471. B. Lobbying seeks to influence a politician or public official on an issue. Public officials cannot lobby themselves, an external influence lobbies the public official.

472. B. *Option B is correct. Stender v. Lucky Stores, Inc. was a class action brought on behalf of women employees of Lucky Stores, Inc. The district court issued a lengthy opinion finding that Lucky's employment practices violated federal and state fair employment laws.*

473. B. *TIPS stand for Threaten, Interrogate, Promise and Spy which represent employer prohibited labor activities.*

474. A. *The Rehabilitation Act of 1973 prohibits discrimination on the basis of disability in programs run by <u>federal agencies</u> (not all agencies); programs that receive federal financial assistance; in federal employment; and in the employment practices of federal contractors.*

475. C. *Hot-cargo agreements are outlawed by the LMRDA or Landrum-Griffin Act of 1959, they are agreements in which employers voluntarily agree with unions not to handle, use, or deal in goods of other employers produced by nonunion employees.*

476. C. *Option A, B and D are crucial to a repatriation program but it is optional to help the employee's spouse gain employment not crucial.*

477. A. *Featherbedding made illegal by the Taft-Hartley Act of 1947 and occurs when an employer deliberately limits production or retains excess staff in order to create jobs or prevent unemployment, typically as a result of a union contract.*

478. B. *The Human Resource Information System (HRIS) will help against promotion discrimination claims, if it can provide data on affirmative action and performance evaluation.*

479. D. *Option A, B and C are instances of unlawful picketing. Also, A union picket an employer to force it to stop doing business with another employer who is the primary target of a labor dispute and at worksites with more than one employer, picketing is only permitted if the protest is clearly directed exclusively at the primary employer.*

480. A. *Consistent reinforcement of competences and skills learnt on the job is critical to an effective transfer of training.*

481. C. *Option A and B are correct explanations of yellow-dog contracts. Yellow Dog contracts are illegal due to the Norris-LaGuardia Act of 1932.*

482. B. *The ADA Amendments Act of 2008 (ADAAA) does not classify current illegal users of drugs as "individuals with disabilities". However, persons addicted to drugs, but <u>who are no longer using drugs illegally</u> and are receiving treatment for drug addiction or who have been rehabilitated successfully, are protected by the ADA from discrimination on the basis of past drug addiction.*

483. C. *The NLRB may seek make-whole remedies, such as reinstatement and backpay for discharged workers, and informational remedies, such as the posting of a notice by the employer promising to not violate the law but the agency cannot change company ownership or assess penalties.*

484. B. *Training cost per employee is calculated by dividing the total training costs by the full-time equivalent employees; $5,000+$1,000=$6,000. The full-time equivalent employees are the 30 full-time employees (because they work 40 hours/week) and 2 of the part-time employees because out of 4 part-time employees who work 20 hours, only 2 can be full-time equivalent of 40 hours/week. Therefore, $6,000/32 full-time eq. employees = $187.50.*

485. D. *A ULP does not disband a union, only a decertification does. A decertification begins when at least 30% of the workers sign cards or a petition asking the NLRB to conduct an decertification election. Unless a majority of the votes cast in the election are in favor of union representation, the union will be decertified.*

486. A. *A sample is a subset containing the characteristics of a larger population. Samples are used in statistical testing when population sizes are too large for the test to include all members.*

487. B. *An unfair labor practice charge must be filed with the NLRB within six months of the date of the occurrence.*

488. D. *An intrinsic reward is an intangible reward of recognition, a sense of achievement, or a conscious satisfaction. Intrinsic rewards arise from within, e.g. the satisfaction of a job well done.*

489. B. *Of all the options, union organizing is the most plausible explanation.*

490. A. *The Age Discrimination in Employment Act (ADEA) makes it unlawful for employers to discharge an individual on the basis of his or her age. The ADEA, however, includes an exception that allows state and local governments to set mandatory retirement ages (usually over 55 years) for firefighters and law enforcement officers.*

491. C. *Petitions are made to the NLRB for elections in the union recognition process, not the LMRA/Taft-Hartley Act, which is a law not a labor board.*

492. D. *Direct compensation refers to the monetary benefits received for work done for a specific duration. Indirect compensation is the name given to the more casual term-employee benefits.*

493. A. *To start the election process, a petition and associated documents must be filed, with the nearest NLRB Regional Office showing support for the petition from at least 30% of employees.*

494. A. *Strategic planning is an organization's process of defining its direction, and making decisions on allocating its resources to pursue same. It is a top-level process done by senior executives not by HR and is not subject to an HR Audit.*

495. B. *A 'neutrality agreement" is a contract between a union and an employer under which the employer agrees to support a union's attempt to organize its workforce.*

496. C. *Indirect compensation is an optional, non-wage compensation provided to employees in addition to their normal wages or salaries. These types of benefits may include group insurance (health, dental, vision, life etc.), disability income protection, retirement benefits and vacation.*

497. D. *In a card check election, the employer agrees to recognize the Union as the official bargaining agent of the employees once the NLRB verifies that a majority of the entire group of employees has signed Union membership cards.*

498. C. *Waivers of ADEA rights and claims require that the individual be given a period of at least 21 days within which to consider the agreement BUT if a waiver is requested in connection with an exit incentive or other employment termination program offered to a group or class of employees, the individual is given a period of at least 45 days within which to consider the agreement.*

499. A. *A bargaining unit is determined when the unit shares a community of interests in wages, hours, and other conditions of employment. In the Sturgis case, the NLRB used a "community of interest test" to ascertain that temporary employees have enough mutual interest with regular employees in wages, scheduling and working conditions to form a collective bargaining unit.*

500. A. *It is imperative to differentiate jobs so as to reward people in roles that make valuable contributions.*

References.

1. https://www.dol.gov/general/topic/benefits-leave/fmla
2. http://www.hr.ucdavis.edu/compensation/labor_market.html
3. http://www.investopedia.com/terms/c/cashbalancepensionplan.asp
4. https://www.law.cornell.edu/uscode/text/15/1681a

5. http://work.chron.com/types-osha-violations-10693.html
6. http://www.investopedia.com/terms/d/dodd-frank-financial-regulatory-reform-bill.asp
7. https://en.wikipedia.org/wiki/Reverse_discrimination
8. http://definitions.uslegal.com/c/contract-bar-doctrine/
9. https://www.eeoc.gov/eeoc/history/35th/thelaw/supreme_court.html
10. Reed, Sandra M., and Anne M. Bogardus. PHR/SPHR: Professional in Human Resources Certification Study Guide. 4th ed. Indianapolis, Ind.: John Wiley & Sons, 2012.

Made in the USA
San Bernardino, CA
27 March 2018